JULIA D ATKINSON

JULIA D ATKINSON

GIGANTIC CHICKENS
WITH FIREWORKS IN THEIR MOUTHS

COMIC AND CURIOUS CLIPPINGS
FROM THE LEGENDARY THEATRICAL PAPER

THE ERA
1860 – 1870

COMPILED BY

JULIA D ATKINSON

JULIA D ATKINSON

Copyright © 2018 Julia D Atkinson

All rights reserved.

ISBN: 978-1-9997610-5-9
ISBN-13: 1-9997610-5-7

GIGANTIC CHICKENS WITH FIREWORKS IN THEIR MOUTHS

THEATRICAL DISPUTE – COURT OF COMMON PLEAS, THURSDAY.
FALSE IMPRISONMENT. – MOON V. TOWERS. – This was an action for an assault and false imprisonment, to which the defendant pleaded not guilty. The case was tried before Mr Justice Williams on the 19th April last.

It appeared at the trial that the plaintiff was the property-master, and the defendant was the proprietor, of the Victoria Theatre, and on last Boxing-night the Pantomime of *Harlequin King Pippin; or, the Enchanted Chicken*, was produced, in which appeared several gigantic chickens with fireworks issuing from their mouths against the Clown, Pantaloon, and all the performers, frightening the whole of them off the stage and remaining sole occupants of the enchanted hills and valleys, and still belching forth volleys of fireworks, to the extreme delight of the admiring audience, when a quantity of blue and other fires appeared, and the enchanted chickens are carried off in a volume of smoke. These fireworks it was the duty of the plaintiff to purchase, which he did, and took receipts for the amounts so expended by him. As the Pantomime did not take so well as was expected, it was determined that a new piece should be added to it, in which also fireworks were introduced, which greatly increased the expenses of the theatre, and he was discharged by the defendant for having expended too much money. The defendant's son, who was the treasurer of the theatre, afterwards went to the plaintiff's house with a policeman, and gave him in charge for defrauding the defendant, his father. He was taken before the magistrate at the Southwark Police-court, when he was remanded for a week, and upon the further hearing of the case, the magistrates discharged him.

The defence was, that the defendant never authorised his son to give the plaintiff in charge, and after hearing the evidence, the jury returned a verdict for the plaintiff – damages, £20.

Subsequently a rule *nisi* was obtained by Mr Hawkins, Q.C., on the part of the defendant, calling upon the plaintiff to show why the verdict should not be set aside, and a new trial had, on the ground that the verdict was against the weight of evidence.

After hearing the arguments of the learned counsel on both sides, their lordships said they were of the opinion that the son had not the authority of the defendant to give the plaintiff into custody; therefore, the defendant could not be made liable, and the judgement would be for the defendant.

The Era, 27th May, 1860

JULIA D ATKINSON

CONTENTS

ACKNOWLEDGEMENTS......ii

1 – 1860: GREEN PAINT OF A POISONOUS NATURE......1

2 – 1861: PIECES WERE MURDERED EVERY NIGHT......6

3 – 1862: A USEFUL LOT OF FADED FINERY......13

4 – 1863: CLAMBERING UP THE CARYATIDES......16

5 – 1864: A SEVERE BLOW WITH AN UMBRELLA......23

6 – 1865: WHAT JOLLY DOGS ARE WE!......29

7 – 1866: UNIQUE FISH DRESSES......37

8 – 1867: ACROBATIC FATHERS, BE KIND TO YOUR KIDS......45

9 – 1868: ONE HIDEOUS JUMBLE......59

10 – 1869: EIGHT INCHES LESS THAN TOM THUMB......79

11 – 1870: I'LL GIVE UP ACTING AND TRY THE POLICE TRICK......92

INDEX......97

ABOUT THE AUTHOR......101

JULIA D ATKINSON

ACKNOWLEDGEMENTS

Many thanks to the British Newspaper Archive for making *The Era*, and many other fascinating vintage newspapers, available online.

The cover was designed by Maduranga Sampath of MSN Art Studio.

The back cover image is a photograph of Lydia Thompson in the title role of the burlesque *Robinson Crusoe* (*circa* 1870). This work is in the public domain in its country of origin and other countries and areas where the copyright term is the author's life plus 70 years or less.

This work is in the public domain the United States because it meets three requirements:
1)it was first published outside the United States (and not published in the U.S. within 30 days),
2)it was first published before 1 March 1989 without copyright notice or before 1964 without copyright renewal or before the source country established copyright relations with the United States,
3)it was in the public domain in its home country (United Kingdom) on the URAA date (January 1, 1996 for most countries).

JULIA D ATKINSON

1
1860
GREEN PAINT OF A POISONOUS NATURE

THE Police Court at Hanley, in the Potteries, Staffordshire, presented an amusing scene on Monday last, from the eccentric and well-known Valentine Vousden being brought before the Bench of Magistrates to account for his erratic conduct on the preceding Saturday evening, and for the more serious offence of threatening to take the life of Police Inspector Cole. It appears that this talented performer is a native of Hanley, and after a most successful professional tour in Ireland, by which he realized about £2,000, he determined to visit the scene of his youthful aspirations, where, "flushed with success," his flow of spirits overpowered the sober proprieties of his sober friends. When at the Albion Inn, amongst other vagaries, he offered to make a gentleman present a gift of his watch, which not being accepted, he endeavoured to force it into the pocket of the party, and during the friendly struggle the watch was lost. He then became so unmanageable that the police were sent for, who, with some trouble, took him to the station-house, where, on being searched, £327 in silver and gold were found on him, which was placed in the care of Inspector Cole.

It appeared that about a month since defendant called at the Police Office and inquired for Inspector Cole, who was not then present, but met the defendant as he was coming out. He asked, "Is that you, Cole; it's my intention to take your life." Cole inquired what he meant, and then Vousden replied, "I shall, and I shall follow you to your grave; and I shall not leave you till I have done that." Complainant had met defendant in the street afterwards, who had taken no notice of him, so that he was at a loss to know his motive for wishing to take his life. Defendant pleaded that he had changed a cheque at the bank and had a glass of wine, which proved too much for him. He had no motive for threatening the Inspector's life, of course it was the fault of the wine.

The defendant, having been bound in £50 to keep the peace, was discharged, with advice to be careful about taking his wine in future.

19/2/1860

DAN RICE thus announces the appearance of a wonderful actress, the renowned Elephant, Lalla Rookh, in the spectacle *The Elephant of Siam*:– "She is a native of the East Indies, and cannot speak a word of the English language, yet her pantomimic powers are so admirable that she is able to sustain the principal character in a heavy spectacle, and make herself as thoroughly understood as if she were thoroughly familiar with our mother tongue. Of a fine figure, somewhat *en bon point*, and a stately carriage, she makes a splendid appearance upon the stage. She dances with considerable grace, and is *au fait* in the details of her profession. The most extraordinary qualification of this wonderful actress, however, is her amazing strength, which exceeds that of the strongest man, and by the ingenuity of the dramatist, her powers in this particular are exhibited in a striking light, and made the important point in working out the development of the plot. She will appear in the new and gorgeous Eastern spectacle now in preparation at the great show, and which will be produced during the present month."

4/3/1860

VICISSITUDES IN THE LIFE OF A BALLET GIRL. – On Wednesday an inquest was held, before Mr C.J. Carttar, coroner, at the Druids' Arms, Greenwich, on the body of Alfred Arthur Langden, aged two years. From the evidence given, it appeared that the mother of the deceased, a young woman nineteen years of age, was a native of Madrid, and followed the occupation of a ballet dancer at the London theatres. She had placed the deceased and another child, now eight months old, to nurse with a woman at Greenwich in December last, and kept up her payments with tolerable punctuality till Easter last, when her engagement at a metropolitan theatre ceasing, she was deprived of the usual means of support for herself and children. On Thursday last the nurse, named Thurnell, the wife of a Greenwich pensioner, was compelled, in order to obtain proper nourishment for the deceased and the other child, to have recourse to the relieving officer. On the following day (Friday) the mother sent a Post-office order to the nurse for 10s., being the whole amount she had been able to obtain during a period of four weeks. On Sunday last, while being fed, the deceased, as was thought, was taken in a fit, and almost instantly expired.

A post-mortem examination of the body, which presented a very emaciated appearance, and weighed scarcely more than 10lb., was ordered by the coroner; and the evidence of Mr Hollingsworth, surgeon, proved that death had resulted from suffocation, the deceased having, it is supposed, from long want of proper nourishment, been so voracious in its swallowing that, in its weakly and debilitated state, it had not sufficient power to relieve itself of food placed in its mouth, which, with the stomach, was found full after death. The other child was also in so emaciated a condition that it was at once taken to the Greenwich Union, where it now remains.

The mother, who was in the inquest-room, was interrogated by the coroner, and stated that the father of the child now living was a medical student at the London University Hospital, but had not contributed towards its support. The father of the deceased, who was a person in a "respectable" position of life, had not furnished her with any means towards its support during the last twelve months. The jury returned a verdict in accordance with the medical testimony.

6/5/1860

An English Actor in Canada Sentenced to be Hanged.

A PRIVATE letter from Canada West contains particulars of a very sad occurrence, which has placed Mr Mackay, son of the celebrated dramatic delineator of Scotch character, in the position of a malefactor, condemned to suffer, on the 7th of June, the extreme penalty of the law for murder. The unfortunate man was himself a pantomimic and general actor of some merit, having played "Pantaloon" in the Haymarket Christmas Pantomime for a couple of seasons, so recently as two or three years ago. Having subsequently emigrated with his wife to Canada, he quitted the profession of the stage, and took a farm in Renfrew County, West Canada, where they resided until the melancholy mischance – for so we must call it – for which his life is now imperilled, took place. The writer thus describes the circumstances:

"During the winter Mr Mackay was occasionally employed by a magistrate as constable, and it fell to his lot to arrest a desperate character named Thomas Byers. The man offered resistance, and Mr Mackay, in the excitement of the moment, accidentally fired his pistol and shot Byers in the thigh. The man lived three weeks afterwards. This occurred on the 7th of February, since which time Mr Mackay has lain in Perth gaol. He was tried on the 11th April, and, to the horror and astonishment of all who are acquainted with the circumstances, he was found guilty of murder, and now lies under sentence of death for the 7th of June. You will perceive there could be no murder in this case, for previous to the day when the unfortunate accident took place Byers was a perfect stranger to Mr Mackay. The judge expressed his surprise how the jury could have arrived at such an extraordinary verdict, and great exertions are being made to procure a remission of the sentence."

The intelligence of the circumstance has given the greatest possible pain to all who remember the many excellent and genial qualities of late Mr Mackay, who may be said to have gained a world-wide celebrity by his personation of the immortal Bailie Nichol Jarvie, of Sir Walter Scott. Moved by every good feeling, a humble and respectful petition to Sir E.W. Head, Governor-General of Canada, has been signed by a large number of our leading citizens, headed by the Lord Provost, praying that his excellency will take the case of the unfortunate Hector Mackay into his merciful consideration, and commute or remit the sentence. The petition left by the mail on Saturday, and we earnestly trust that its prayer may be successful, at least so far as commuting the capital punishment. – *Scotsman*.
Hector Mackay's sentence was subsequently commuted to seven years' imprisonment.
20/5/1860

THEATRICAL DISPUTE – COURT OF COMMON PLEAS, THURSDAY.
FALSE IMPRISONMENT. – MOON V. TOWERS. – This was an action for an assault and false imprisonment, to which the defendant pleaded not guilty. The case was tried before Mr Justice Williams on the 19th April last.

It appeared at the trial that the plaintiff was the property-master, and the defendant was the proprietor, of the Victoria Theatre, and on last Boxing-night the Pantomime of *Harlequin King Pippin; or, the Enchanted Chicken*, was produced, in which appeared several gigantic chickens with fireworks issuing from their mouths against the Clown, Pantaloon, and all the performers, frightening the whole of them off the stage and remaining sole occupants of the enchanted hills and valleys, and still belching forth volleys of fireworks, to the extreme delight of the admiring audience, when a quantity of blue and other fires appeared, and the enchanted chickens are carried off in a volume of smoke. These fireworks it was the duty of the plaintiff to purchase, which he did, and took receipts for the amounts so expended by him. As the Pantomime did not take so well as was expected, it was determined that a new piece should be added to it, in which also fireworks were introduced, which greatly increased the expenses of the theatre, and he was discharged by the defendant for having expended too much money. The defendant's son, who was the treasurer of the theatre, afterwards went to the plaintiff's house with a policeman, and gave him in charge for defrauding the defendant, his father. He was taken before the magistrate at the Southwark Police-court, when he was remanded for a week, and upon the further hearing of the case, the magistrates discharged him.

The defence was, that the defendant never authorised his son to give the plaintiff in charge, and after hearing the evidence, the jury returned a verdict for the plaintiff – damages, £20.

Subsequently a rule *nisi* was obtained by Mr Hawkins, Q.C., on the part of the defendant, calling upon the plaintiff to show why the verdict should not be set aside, and a new trial had, on the ground that the verdict was against the weight of evidence.

After hearing the arguments of the learned counsel on both sides, their lordships said they were of the opinion that the son had not the authority of the defendant to give the plaintiff into custody; therefore, the defendant could not be made liable, and the judgement would be for the defendant.
27/5/1860

ACCIDENT TO MISS VANDENHOFF. – On Tuesday evening last, as the above lady was descending from the stage of the Northampton Theatre to her dressing-room, she trod upon some slippery substance, which precipitated her with fearful velocity down several steps, straining the ligaments of the left knee. We regret to state, although this mischance is not so serious as it might have been, that it will deprive the stage, for some time at least, of one of its brightest ornaments.
Miss Vandenhoff died of inflammation of the brain two months later.
3/6/1860

Melancholy Death of the Scenic Artist of the Theatre Royal, Brighton.

CONSIDERABLE gloom was cast over the theatrical circles at Brighton on Thursday morning, by the announcement of the sudden death on the previous evening of Mr Joseph Wilson, for several years past principal scenic artist to the Theatre Royal.

It appears that about ten days since Mr Wilson was engaged in preparing some transparencies, in which green paint of a poisonous nature was required, and it is supposed that whilst using this he inadvertently placed the brush in his mouth for a few seconds. Shortly afterwards he was troubled with what appeared to be a boil inside his lip, but for a time he thought little of it, until becoming worse, medical aid was at last called in; but the subtle poison had been allowed too long to perform its deadly office, and though hopes were entertained until about six o'clock on Wednesday evening, of his recovery, he about that time became suddenly worse, and died between eight and nine o'clock. He was a young man rising rapidly in his profession, and much respected by all those who came in contact with him. He was not altogether unknown in London, as he was formerly engaged at the Olympic Theatre. He has left a widow (in ill-health and within two months of her confinement) and four children utterly unprovided for. A subscription has been commenced for them, and we are requested to state that Mr H. Nye Chart, the lessee of the Theatre Royal, will gladly receive donations thereto; and any sums sent to Mr F. Ledger, THE ERA office, Catherine Street, Strand, will be thankfully received, duly acknowledged, and properly applied for the benefit of the widow and children.

19/8/1860

EXTRAORDINARY BREACH OF CONTRACT AND ITS RESULTS.

Howes' and Cushing's American Circus visited Dumfries on Monday, and gave two exhibitions in a large marquee on the Dock-park. At the evening exhibition something like a riot arose by the refusal by the manager to pay a sovereign to anyone who would ride a mule three times round the ring without being thrown off. A lad named William Quin, who is in the employment of Mr William Teenan, horse dealer, Dumfries, undertook the feat, and insisted that he had ridden the mule three times round the ring and kept his seat, notwithstanding that the reins had been cut by one of the Circus people, and everything had been done to prevent his succeeding in the trial. The manager, on the other hand, averred that Quin had not ridden in jockey fashion, had nearly choked the animal by clutching it round the neck, and had only ridden round the ring twice, a portion of the spectators having interfered. Quin's claims were loudly backed by a large number of the audience, and a mighty uproar was the result, in which some of the benches were smashed. Quin stuck to the mule, and proceeded to take it away home with him, followed by an immense crowd, cheering and yelling in a state of great excitement, and evidently anxious to ascertain the whereabouts of the manager, who had left the Circus for his lodgings. The superintendent of police, Mr Mitchell, was obliged to take steps for quelling the disturbance. The money was ultimately paid to Quin, the mule restored, and the streets soon resumed their wonted quiet. At the last visit of this Circus to Dumfries a similar occurrence took place. The lad Quin on that occasion also claimed to have won the money, which he did not get. This, no doubt, on the present occasion, gave additional energy to the remonstrances of the crowd.

16/9/1860

A JESTER IN TROUBLE. – At the Leeds Town Hall, on Tuesday, Mr W.F. Wallett, whose quips and cranks have lightened many a sad heart, appeared in a novel character of a defendant in a charge of assault preferred by a labourer named George Laverack.

Mr Wallett, as the manager of the Alhambra Theatre Company, has recently been performing in Leeds, and it appeared that on Monday evening week the complainant went to enjoy the puns and witticisms of the great Jester, but instead of enjoying his *otium cum dignitate** in peace, he rushed into trouble. Being in that happy state of inebriation when the heart offers services which the hand cannot perform, he volunteered his aid in bearing the performing bull on his pedestal of glory, and carrying him round the ring. His unsteadiness grew into strength as the audience rent the air with their plaudits, but whilst restoring the bull to his natural sphere, his weakness returned, he stumbled, and got his foot crushed by the platform. The defendant, liberal in the buoyancy of his humour, ordered him to be sent to a doctor, and undertook the responsibility of paying all expenses.

The injuries were dressed, and in a few days the complainant had recovered, but he had paid 3s. 6d., and he resolved to appeal to Mr Wallett to refund the amount. Mr Wallett having already paid too dearly for the volunteer service of an obtrusive spectator, refused to pay more, and the complainant becoming importunate and insulting, he, according to Laverack's statement, took up a basin of water and threw it in his face, remarking "that is the way I pay." This was the assault complained of, and it was indignantly denied by Mr Wallett, who was corroborated by a police-officer who was on duty at the Circus, upon which the case was discharged, the complainant being ordered to pay the costs.

Leisure with dignity.
21/10/1860

WE have this week to record the demise of a well-known stage favourite, who, in his time, played many parts, for which even our greatest histrionic artists would find themselves but incompetent representatives. The famous Newfoundland dog "Nelson," (the property of Mr S. Wild, the theatrical manager), died on Saturday, November 3rd, in his seventeenth year. Among the good actions of his life must be recorded the fact that he saved a man from drowning in the River Ribble, at Preston, on the 6th of June, 1849, and for which a silver medal was bestowed. The deceased Nelson was considered one of the best performing dogs in England, and he had the honour of being written for by several minor authors, who developed his sagacity in pieces suited to his canine talents. His death, which occurred at Blackburn, will be much regretted by those to whom his good qualities had rendered him greatly attached.

11/11/1860

AN incident occurred in the railway station in Edinburgh, on Tuesday last, which created no small degree of amusement and alarm to many persons who happened to be present. The troupe of lions, lately performing at Sanger's Circus, being engaged to perform at Astley's, of course some mode of conveyance was necessary to transport the leonine baggage; and, as haste was a most important feature in the case, nothing could possibly be thought of more accommodating than the 2pm mail train. Unfortunately, some of the other passengers took alarm, and objected to travel in company with their four-footed friends. The officials, however, were deaf to all entreaties; and, there being no Act of Parliament against any performers, whether biped or quadruped, journeying by rail, the lions were allowed to proceed to their destination with all possible despatch. Some individuals in consequence remained behind, and did not leave Edinburgh until late in the evening.

2/12/1860

2
1861
PIECES WERE MURDERED EVERY NIGHT

IN the Blackburn Workhouse are eighty-two inmates whose united ages amount to 6,153 years, or an average age of seventy-five years and thirteen days. The oldest female, born in 1772, is named Miss Ann Mainley, who, for upwards of fifty years, delighted the busy thousands assembled at the country fairs, she having been an actress at Mr Wild's Travelling Theatre during that long period. The old lady is comfortably housed and well taken care of.
20/1/1861

AN AMAZON. – Mrs Osborne, the wife of a Licensed Victualler in the city, was charged on Friday, at Bow Street Police Court, by Picton, 101 F, the officer on duty in the interior of the Strand Theatre, with assaulting him in the execution of his duty.

The officer deposed: Last evening, just before half-price, several gentlemen left the pit to join their friends in the boxes, and as I knew they were not coming back, I requested the other persons on the same seat to close up, so as to leave room for others who might come in at half-price. The defendant was keeping a place for the gentleman who had accompanied her to the theatre, he having gone out for a short time. She said to me, "You are not going to fill up my seat?" I said, "Certainly not," but requested her to close up, reserving only the seat required for her friend. She then clenched her fist and struck me, saying, "There, take that, though you are a policeman. I have knocked many a man down, and I would knock you down for two pins, if you were as big as a house." As the curtain was then rising, and I did not want to disturb the audience and interrupt the performance, I let the matter drop for the time, and when the piece was over, and she was leaving the house, I took her in charge. The gentleman who was with defendant accompanied us to the station. He was a little the worse for liquor, but defendant was quite sober. She was immediately bailed out.

Defendant admitted that she struck the policeman, saying she was provoked to it in consequence of his having rudely pushed against her. Defendant's husband said that he was sure the defendant would not have struck the constable without provocation; but she was a woman who would defend herself if insulted. Mr Henry – That she has a right to do. But you were not present, were you? – Mr Osborne – No. The business will not allow us to go out together, so a friend of mine kindly consented to take her. The friend here came forward and declared emphatically that he was not the worse for liquor. He had nothing to drink when out of the theatre. Did not go to any public house, but walked about the streets, because he did not care about hearing the play, but preferred taking a walk. Ultimately Mr Henry fined the defendant 20s., which was immediately paid.
27/1/1861

ATTEMPTED SUICIDE OF A PANTALOON IN NOTTINGHAM. – For the past seven weeks Mr Leslie has taken an active part in the successful Pantomime, *The Sleeping Beauty*, as Pantaloon. On Monday evening last, on the termination of the performances, he repaired to his dressing-room, took up a pistol, and lodged the contents of the barrel in his face. Fortunately, the weapon was loaded only with gunpowder, and had not the effect contemplated by the unhappy individual. Medical assistance was shortly rendered, and, upon examination, it was found that he had sustained no serious injury beyond the disfigurement of his face by wadding. The cause of this rash attempt upon his life is owing to disappointed love – his *ladie faire* having jilted him without assigning any reason for her conduct.
10/2/1861

THE MONKEY AND THE MONEY. – A singular circumstance occurred, a few nights ago, at the Equestrian Circus, now at Cheltenham, under the management of Mr J. Myers. A sum of 28s., principally in florins, was suddenly missed from the place in which the money was usually kept, and a "hue and cry" was raised throughout the establishment. Mr J. Kesley, the treasurer, shortly afterwards had occasion to pass a monkey, which belongs to the company, and saw it spit out a florin. Of course, his suspicions were aroused, and, seizing the animal, he was convinced beyond doubt that the remainder of the missing money was deposited in "Jocko's" stomach. A short time elapsed, and he vomited more money, until the whole amount, with the exception of eighteenpence, was returned to the treasury. As a punishment for this little peccadillo, the monkey was put in a box upon which a weight was placed, but the animal, during the night, managed to get his head between the box and the lid, and could not withdraw it, and before his position could be discovered the poor monkey was suffocated. The body has been passed into the hands of Mr Charles Hoskins, for preservation.

TO THE EDITOR OF THE ERA.
Dear Sir, – Wishing to enjoy the inimitable performance of Charles Kean in *Louis XI*, I selected last Friday evening as an opportunity for so doing. I accordingly went to Old Drury, and, having paid my fee for the first circle, was shown (after a little preliminary matter with the box-keeper), to the centre compartment. Seeing the box nearly empty, I was about to descend, in order the better to witness the performance, when I was informed that I could not do so, as all the *vacant* seats were *already filled*, and my position was on the fifth row – back. The band struck up, and concluded. The curtain rose, and the play commenced – *still the other seats were vacant*. In a most interesting part of the play, however, the door of my box was opened for the incomers, and now the *nuisance* began. I had to get off my seat no less than seven times within half-an-hour for the seat-holders to pass, and, in so doing, I missed many of the fine delineations of the great actor, for the witnessing of which I had come expressly. I could not help thinking that the after-comers ought to have forfeited their seats by not being in them before the curtain rose. I have since reflected on the matter, and I would respectfully suggest, for the better comfort of that portion of the public who go to the theatre for the performances, that there should be a rule requiring all seat-holders to be in their respective places by a certain time, on pain of losing their right to the seats so retained for their use. This would not apply, of course, to *private boxes*. – I am, dear Sir, yours faithfully, F.A. LEWIS.
17/2/1861

EDWIN POYNTON, a medical student, living in Goodge Street, was charged before Mr Beadon, at Marlborough Street Police Court, with creating a disturbance at the Queen's Theatre, Tottenham Court Road, and throwing a dead rat in persons' faces. The prisoner, in a half-drunken state, was seen by a man named Baptist, the theatre-keeper, to throw something in the face of a lad in the pit stalls, and on his going down from the upper part of the theatre to stop the disturbance thus created by the prisoner, he found that he had a dead rat, which he had taken from his pocket, and had put in some persons' faces. Baptist then seized him with the view of putting him out, when he struck him, and, in a severe struggle, tore his coat. Mr Beadon said: I'll teach you, young gentlemen, who, instead of being gentlemen, are blackguards, to act better. You will pay a fine of £5, or two months, and if you do a similar thing again, and are brought before me, I will send you for trial. The defendant, who seemed rather displeased at the cost of his silly freak, paid the fine a short time after.

MURDER OF AN ENGLISH CLOWN AT CONSTANTINOPLE. – On Monday evening, a cowardly murder was committed near the Tésé, under circumstances of such trivial provocation as to give the crime an unusual degree of guilty cruelty. Three masquers – one of them a woman – were swaggering noisily down the street in the quarter in question, as Howard, one of the English clowns at Soullier's Circus, and some friends were leaving a cafe in the neighbourhood. The dominoed ruffians, with whom scurrilous license passed for wit, addressed some remark of the former sort to Howard and his companions, to which the Englishman promptly replied. From "chaffing" the word-play soon grew to worse, and, the masquers still coming off second best, one of them sidled up to poor Howard and stabbed him deep into the abdomen before the cowardly intention could be perceived. The ruffians then fled; but, pursuit being made, the woman was seized. Her male companions succeeded in making good their escape down a couple of the narrow and dark lanes in the neighbourhood. The victim of this dastardly act was speedily carried up to the hospital of the Sisters of Charity; but, though every care was there lavished upon him, the poor fellow died during the night. The actual assassin is said to be an Italian, known to the police. One of his associates, a tinker named Marco, and who is believed to have been his companion on Monday evening, is in custody. – *Levant Herald*, Feb. 13th.

DR KAHN ON MARRIAGE. – A New and entirely Re-written Edition (the forty-fifth of this celebrated Treatise, with new Steel Plates, Woodcuts, &c.) is now ready. The object of the Work is not to maintain any particular hypothesis but to enable every one to understand for himself the structure and functions of the organs concerned in the fulfilment of the Physical obligations of the Married State; to acquaint him with the consequences arising from excess; to prevent unnecessary misapprehension from unfounded fears, and to indicate, when these fears are well founded, the means of speedy relief. The work is not crowded with the technicalities of ordinary professional books, nor does it present the crudeness which characterises the so-called "popular works" on the subject. Price One Shilling, free by post for Thirteen Stamps; or in a Sealed Envelope, Twenty-two Stamps, either from the Publisher, J. ALLEN, 20, Warwick Lane; or from the Author's address, 17, Harley Street, Cavendish Square, London. [ADVT.]
3/3/1861

STAGE PLAYS IN UNLICENSED HOUSES.
POOLE PETTY SESSIONS – MARCH 11th.
Magistrates present: The Mayor (E. Lacy, Esq.), E. Mullett, Esq., J. Lankester, Esq.; and J. Gosse, Esq.
 Edward Hymer, landlord of the Ship Inn, Paradise Street, was summoned by Superintendent Inkpen for allowing Stage-plays to be performed in his house, such house not being duly licensed. Mr H.W. Dickinson appeared to support the complaint, and Mr W. Parr appeared for the defence. […]
 The learned advocate (Mr Dickinson) proceeded to read one of the bills, which excited the laughter of the Court. The place was described as "Hymer's Grand Music Hall, Ship Inn, Poole," and Mr Hymer announced in the bill to the inhabitants of Poole, that at an enormous expense he had fitted up and decorated a Temple of Apollo, for their comfort and harmless amusement. He also assured the public that it was not his intention to open this place as a resort for the lowest of society (laughter), but to suit all classes, who had but to pay a visit to satisfy themselves of its comfort and respectability. The bill went on to describe that strict order would be kept, and that he had "succeeded in engaging some of the first talent in England." Then followed a long string of names. First was Mr Robert Farmer, the side-splitting comedian and comic vocalist, from the Theatre Royal, Belfast. This gentleman he intended to call as a witness. […]

P.C. Beaken deposed that on the 22nd February he went to the Ship Inn, in Paradise Street, which is kept by Edward Hymer, it being a licensed public house. On that evening he went to a room upstairs where there was a performance. The money-taker (a female) stood at the door, and took money to admit persons to the room. Witness saw several sailors pay money. There was not a large audience that night. At the end of the room there was a stage. There were curtains to the stage, which were lowered and raised when a bell rang. There were foot-lights to the stage. The Play was something about a slave-dealer. There were three persons on the stage at a time; sometimes one. They were dressed for the occasion. They spoke to each other and acted. Witness considered he was seeing a Play. There was no murder committed while he was there. The performers went on and off the stage several times. Could not say whether it was like great Theatres. Witness had been there on several occasions, and seen different Plays. Witness heard music. All performances that took place were on the stage, and behind the curtain and drapery.

Cross-examined by Mr Parr: The entertainment was not all singing; there was acting, the singing being between the parts. Witness did not see any murder committed – (laughter) – but he saw a young man run away with a young woman. (Renewed laughter.) Witness had seen Mr Farmer, the "side-splitting" comedian, but he did not make his sides split. There was nothing very particular in the performance, and witness thought it rather a tame business. The performers did not wear their ordinary dresses. While witness was present on this occasion, the piece was something about a slave-dealer, and Farmer wore an old straw hat and a white slop. (Loud laughter.)

Robert Farmer, the "side-splitting comedian," was next called, and deposed that he was a comedian and comic vocalist, and had performed at the Gravesend and Dover theatres, and in a travelling booth. He knew Hymer, and had been engaged by him about three weeks before Christmas at a salary of 15s. per week, "to do acting, singing, dancing, and so forth." His wife was engaged, and she was called Miss Sarah Farmer. He had now left Hymer. Hymer had a room or theatre in which theatrical performances were carried on. He performed every night except Sundays, save one or two nights when the room was thrown open for dancing, as only a few boys came to the performance, and they had their money returned. The room was upstairs; it was a very "tidy" room, and had a stage in it. There were foot-lights and float lights, the same as in a Theatre; and there was working scenery, both flats and drop scene. When witness first went there, Mr Sumerfield acted as stage-manager. All the performers went upon the stage, and Mr Hymer, Mrs Hymer, and all the children occasionally. (Laughter). They had a great number at Christmas during the Pantomime. Pieces were murdered every night, so far as that goes; there was a little murder occasionally in every piece except the Farce. They performed a variety of plays, amongst them *Bombastes Furioso*, *The Floating Beacon*, *Ben Bolt*, *Gregory's Blunders*, and *Send Your Wives To Coventry*. Witness remembered the evening of the 22nd of February. On that evening the play was *The Green Hills of the Far West*. Six characters performed, dressed in costume. Witness took the part of a slave-dealer, Jonathan Marsden. Witness's wife performed, but he was not sure Hymer did. The plot of the play was that witness and his friend were two escaped felons. Witness was supposed to be more fortunate than his friend, and gained a little money. Witness wanted to carry off a gentleman's daughter, and his friend assists, and it turns out that she is his friend's sister. (Laughter.) No songs were sung during the Play. There was a Farce, and singing and dancing during the evening. Witness had performed every night that there were plays. This was a stage entertainment, the same as he had seen in other theatres. Witness did not think that any of the performers had any great talents, but they did their best to make it a dramatic performance. Witness was killed that night, as also was Mr Johnson. Witness played in *Ben Bolt* the next night, and Mr Hymer played also. The plot was that a miller sent a man to sea, and then tried to get his wife away from him. (Laughter.) The same thing took place each evening that there was a performance. Everything was done to make a stage entertainment of it. There was music, consisting of a pianoforte, a violin, and two corneteans, played by one man. (Laughter.)

Cross-examined by Mr Parr: You are the celebrated side-splitting comedian, described in the bills as being from the Theatre Royal, Belfast? – Witness – Never was there in my life, sir. (Loud laughter.)

Mr Parr – Did you draw up this description? – Witness – I had nothing to do with it. Mr Sumerfield wrote the bill; it was read to me, and I assented. I liked it very well. (Laughter.) I did not think it a grand thing to come from Belfast. I am not ambitious to get a great name in the Profession. (Laughter.)

Mr Parr: You have not made a very good living here, I believe; your side-splitting comicalities were not very much appreciated? – Witness: I made them laugh a little; but they laughed most at Mr Hymer's Tragedy; he made them laugh when they ought to cry. (Roars of laughter.)

Mr Parr: I believe there was a little bit of Comedy or Tragedy which caused you to leave? – Witness: Well, there was a bit of a scuffle, I believe; the ladies could not agree. Hymer discharged me at a minute's notice.

Mr Parr: Did you know you were doing what was illegal? – Witness: I was quite aware of it; we were like smugglers, and ran the risk. I expected every minute, when I saw a policeman come in, to be dragged off the stage to prison. (Laughter.)

Mr Parr: Then it is no wonder you could not cut your comicalities, when you were afraid of a gentleman in blue? – Witness: I was rather at a disadvantage.

Mr Parr: You are the person who has given this information? – Witness – I must get a living somehow. I have had to beg my bread lately and that is rather hard upon one in the Theatrical Profession.

Examination continued: I have been accustomed to Music Halls. There was music there, and also curtains and a stage. There are a great many at Portsmouth, and they are all liable. *The Green Hills of the Far West* was got up by Mr Johnson. We take a part from the book, and make up our own language. We are such excellent actors it is no difficulty for us to make up our own language. (Laughter.) *Ben Bolt* is a play written in a book. We have a plot to work from. We must have one, because we are not so clever as to make up a piece out of our heads. There was murder committed every night; I was disgusted at it. The people laughed enough at Mr Hymer playing the Idiot Boy. (Laughter.)

Mr Parr, for the defence, contended that these were not Stage-plays at all, and if those people had been called upon to furnish a copy of their plays they could not have done so because none existed, the words they used being of their own invention. The witness Farmer had got hold of the word "plot" no doubt from having seen in the newspapers lately that it was necessary to have a plot to commence a Stage-play, and had asserted that the performances at this place were founded on a plot, while such did not appear to be the case. A great deal had been made about footlights and scenery, but there was really nothing in it. The same was the case in every music hall in the metropolis and elsewhere, and no one for a moment ventured to say that Stage-plays were performed there. […]

The Bench having consulted, the Mayor said there was no difference in the opinion of the magistrates to the defendant having performed Stage-plays. The fixed the penalty of £5 with full costs, with the intimation that if any further performance took place of any licensed Play, Farce, Burletta, or part of any Play, the full penalty of £20 per night would be exacted; and if any Plays not duly licensed by the Lord Chamberlain were performed, the full penalty of £50 would be enforced.

The Bench allowed the defendant twenty-four hours to pay, and if not paid at that time, the sum to be levied on his goods, and in default of sufficient distraint he was to be committed to prison for two months.

17/3/1861

M. Blondin's Old Tricks.
TO THE EDITOR OF THE ERA.
Sir, – Two of your contemporaries, in eulogising the performance of the Frenchman at the Crystal Palace, on the *corde ordinaire* of a rope dancer, speak of the feats of playing the violin and beating the drum as marvellous. I am, therefore, compelled, in common justice, to inform you, and (I trust) your readers that these tricks are a piracy on my performance, of which they are a lame and unfinished imitation, copied from me during my first engagement at Niblo's, New York, which extended from May

12th to December 15th, 1856. The popularity which I attained throughout the American Union was, perhaps, the cause of the party in question coming 200 miles to see me execute the feats that I am proud to see termed marvellous by your two contemporaries in their critiques of the Crystal Palace rope-dancing. The original performer of an overture on the violin whilst turning somersaults on the tight rope is my eldest brother (now retired, and residing at Cheltenham), which feat, together with *my* original *Drum Polka*, was performed by me at the City of London Theatre in April, 1855, and which, not withstanding the absence of Yankee puffing and profuse advertising, gained some golden opinions from yourself and contemporaries. You may, sir, perhaps remember that I sustained a Shakespearian character on alternate nights with those performances. As to such tricks on the rope as baskets, stilts, sacks, barrows, clogs, &c., &c., they have long since been discarded by anyone professing to be an *artiste*. They are only fit for the *French Fête Booth*, from whence they came, and were done by my father at the Surrey, Olympic, &c., *fifty years ago*. May I hope, sir, that you will give this a corner in your columns, where justice is accorded to all Professionals; and asking pardon for intruding upon your time and space, I am, Sir, with all respect, yours truly, JOHN MILTON HENGLER, George Hotel, Burton on Trent, July 2nd.
7/7/1861

AN UNFORTUNATE WEDDING. – Mr Emidy, the proprietor of the Circus now performing at Maidstone, had with his troupe a young girl named Brierly, who was an apprentice, duly bound to be taught the equestrian art for six years, two years of which had passed, and the lady, being talented, had become worth £5 per week to her master. Mr Emidy had also a troupe of bounding Arabs, one of whom, named Hassam, was smitten with the fair one, and on Friday last went with her to the registrar's office, and was united in the bonds of matrimony, the Arab taking his wife home. He was not long permitted to enjoy his felicity, for Mr Emidy, who could not afford to lose his apprentice, upon whom he had bestowed much time and trouble, applied to the magistrates, who granted a warrant for her apprehension, and the new-made wife passed the remainder of the day and night in the dreary cells of the police-station. The penalty of the indenture was £180, but the matter was ultimately pecuniarily arranged between the husband, who is a very respectable fellow, and Mr Emidy, and the following day the apprenticeship was put an end to, and the wife again restored to her husband.
14/7/1861

KEYZOR and BENDON'S TWO-GUINEA BINOCULAR OPERA GLASS sent carriage-free on receipt of Post-office Order to any part of the United Kingdom. The extraordinary power of this instrument renders it adapted to answer the combined purposes of telescope and opera glass; it will define objects distinctly at ten miles distance; it is suitable for the Theatre, Race Course, Sportsmen Tourists, and general outdoor observations. Only to be obtained of KEYZOR and BENDON (successors to Harris and Son), opticians, 60, HIGH HOLBORN, W.C. Illustrated price lists of Optical and mathematical instruments free on receipt of two stamps.
21/7/1861

PUNCH AND JUDY AT A DISCOUNT IN OXFORD. – On Thursday evening the proprietor of a Punch and Judy establishment announced at the close of his performance in the High Street that, after obtaining the very gracious permission of the Right Worshipful the Mayor to perform "for one day, and for one day only," his receipts amounted to 3d., which he intended to spend in cakes for Toby, after which he should leave this ancient and loyal city with disgust, and betake himself to Witney, Woodstock, Danbury, or some such spirited places, where the people had sense to appreciate, and means to encourage native talent.
1/9/1861

MR COXWELL, the distinguished aeronaut, and the Messrs Pearson Jun., of Lawton Hall, near Congleton, are now progressing, we are happy to say, towards complete recovery.

It will be remembered that on August 19th, a descent took place during a violent wind, on the stone-walled and rocky locality near Brierlow toll-gate, about two-and-a-half miles from Buxton. A valley favourable for alighting had been missed, owing to the force of the wind, and the car not being over-stocked with ballast, the voyageurs found themselves skimming over the "back-bone of England," the wild rugged surface of which is in every way objectionable to a balloon. Mr Coxwell seeing no possible mode of evading a rough landing, prepared for the worst, and placed his passengers in the safest possible position, viz., at the bottom of either side of the basket, where hand-ropes are placed by which to hold in emergencies like this. As the grapnel (a large, powerful instrument, 42lbs.), trailed along the ground, it glided over the soil and tore down stone walls, as if there were no holding ground or material for it to take effect in. The consequence was that the car was brought down in contact with the walls, and the only remedy was to exhaust the gas as quickly as possible, and lessen the number of concussions. It was here manifestly that the experienced aeronaut was equal to the occasion, as he peremptorily kept his companions well down in the basket, and told them that if they attempted to move or get out they would be killed on the spot.

Fortunately, the Messrs Pearson are remarkably endowed with what is styled pluck, and they stuck to the ship and obeyed Mr Coxwell's orders to the letter. It was now the critical moment – two or three severe bumps were inevitable, the wind blowing in angry gusts, and the car dashed through one wall of about eighteen inches in thickness, making a clear breach, and hurling the stones forward as if they had been pounded by the largest Armstrong missile at present in use. Mr Coxwell was full strain on the upper valve, which is thirty inches in diameter, but still the mass bore onward, and a second clean breach was repeated in the next wall. Away again with renewed vigour, and down for the third time, and once again through another wall, and now the cry was raised by astounded lookers-on that two fields further lay the Deep Dale or gorge, which would surely prove fatal. Happily, the fourth wall having been dashed down, and a considerable quantity of gas lost – the balloon itself caught some of the stones and tore from bottom to top – several countrymen, especially the sons of the toll-bar keeper, now rushed to the rescue. Mr Coxwell despatched a messenger for a conveyance to take them to the Royal Hotel, at Buxton, where they arrived in due time and received the best medical attention that could be procured. The injuries sustained were: Mr T. Pearson, fracture of the skull; Mr A. Pearson, injuries to the head and broken fore-arm; and Mr Coxwell, bruised and cut from head to foot, with a bad contused wound on the right thigh. This, we believe, is the first personal accident that has ever befallen Mr Coxwell out of nearly four hundred ascensions. – *Buxton Advertiser*, September 7th.
15/9/1861

ON Monday night (says the *Caledonian Mercury*) a most humorous, though in a sense disagreeable incident occurred in the Queen's Theatre in the opera of *Norma*. In the Second Act, when Norma reproaches Pollio for his infidelity, and where the latter rushes after the former towards the gong, Mdlle Tietjens, in her impatience to strike the "sacred bronze," that "a new victim" might be revealed to the assembled Druids, Bards, and Warriors, by some mischance brought the mallet in contact with the nasal organ of Signor Giuglini as Pollio, and made a bleeding victim of him on the spot. The accident was not observed until a minute or two afterwards, and when the Signor, from loss of blood, had to retire. The fair cantatrice, evidently much disconcerted, could not proceed, and the curtain suddenly dropped, greatly to the astonishment of the audience, few of whom had noticed the occurrence. Mr Wyndham immediately appeared, and explained that a slight accident had occurred to Signor Guiglini; and in a few minutes the Signor presented himself again, and, with the blushing priestess, brought the Opera to a brilliant close.
10/11/1861

3
1862
A USEFUL LOT OF FADED FINERY

ON Friday evening week two Pantomimic accidents occurred – one at Drury Lane Theatre and the other at the Victoria Theatre, which fortunately, however, were not fatal. At Drury Lane, Mr Huline, the Clown, in firing a pistol at the Pantaloon, Mr Tanner, misdirected it, and unfortunately wounded the lean and slippered gentleman above the eye and on the cheek, but not seriously. At the Victoria Theatre, behind the scenes, there was an escape of gas, and considering the extent of the explosion, it is a perfect miracle that the whole edifice was not enveloped in flames.
5/1/1862

PUPIL FOR THE STAGE. – A Lady or Gentleman desirous of studying for the Theatrical Profession, can be fully instructed by Mr COE, Stage-Director at the Theatre Royal, Haymarket. Mr Coe gives Private Lessons in Elocution, Intonation, and graceful gesticulation. 7, Jermyn Street, St James's, S.W.
19/1/1862

Fracas on the Stage of the Victoria Theatre.
Samuel Lockyer, an active-looking man, described on the charge-sheet as an actor, was brought on Monday before Mr Burcham at the Southwark Police Court, by Herrington, the officer of the Victoria Theatre, charged with committing a violent and unprovoked assault on Mr Isaac Cohen on the stage of the above theatre.

Mr Cohen, whose right jaw was much swollen, said that he was Stage Director of the Victoria Theatre, and the prisoner was engaged as the Sprite in the Pantomime. On Saturday night, during the first scene of the comic business, the prisoner had to go through a kind of drawing-room entertainment with his two sons, who were very young. In the course of their tumbling and jumping the defendant performed in such a clumsy manner that the audience hissed them off the stage. Witness was at that time attending to his duties on the stage, when he saw the defendant knocking one of the lads about in an unmerciful manner, and dragging him up some stairs. Witness thought it his duty to interfere for the protection of the lad, and, while he was endeavouring to get the latter away, the defendant struck him such a tremendous blow on the right jaw that he firmly believed that it was broken.

Mr Burcham asked whether he knocked him down? – Witness replied that he fell against a wall, and was stunned for some moments.

In answer to the charge, the defendant said he was extremely sorry for what had occurred, and was willing to make an ample apology to Mr Cohen.

Mr Burcham observed that he supposed it was necessary that he should be perfectly steady when he went through that hazardous performance with his sons.

Mr Cohen said that it was, and his being under the influence of liquor endangered their lives and limbs. Not only that, but the audience were disappointed.

Mr Burcham said that the conduct of the defendant was very bad indeed. The performance of itself was extremely hazardous, and required a great deal of hard training before before they could accomplish those feats; therefore, his lads ought not to be treated in such a brutal way. Mr Cohen had acted kindly in going to the protection of one of them, and then he was attacked, and his jaw nearly broken. Defendant must pay a penalty of 40s. for the assault on Mr Cohen, or go to prison for fourteen days.

The prisoner paid the fine.
26/1/1862

ON Saturday evening the performances at the Lyceum were suspended for a few minutes by Miss Lydia Thompson, the favourite actress and dancer at this establishment, going off into strong hysterics under the influence evidently of painful emotions, soon after she had made her entrance as the heroine of the Extravaganza. Mr Spencer came forward, and soliciting the indulgence of the audience for a short time, explained the cause of the interruption. It would seem that the same morning a letter had been received by the young lady at the Theatre, stating that in the course of the evening a pistol would be fired at her, and that she was to be prepared for the immediate termination of her career on earth. Judging by the feeling expressed by those who heard this statement, the anonymous author of the threatening epistle would have received a summary punishment for his unmanly conduct had he been detected amongst the audience.
2/3/1862

SPIRIT-RAPPING. – The world has recently been startled by the account given in a leading journal of the wonderful revelations said to have been given by "departed spirits" from an unknown world. We would advise all searchers after truth, who may have been impressed by this delusion, to pay a visit to the Colosseum, where they will hear explained, and see the so-called manifestations carried out before them, viz., the names on paper pellets, the wonderful appearance of writing on the arm, &c., &c. The very admirable manner in which the matter is treated by Mr Taylor, and the fearlessness with which he exposes the tricks practised by these mediums, is deserving of much praise, and cannot fail to convince even the most credulous how easily they may be deceived.
30/3/1862

WE regret to hear that Mrs Mackney, so many years a deserved favourite at the City, Standard, Britannia, and Victoria Theatres, in passing down the New Cut, Lambeth, slipped over some cucumber rind, with which the pavements in that locality are continually strewn, and broke her wrist in four places, dislocated her left arm, and, unfortunately, has lost an excellent engagement with Mr Howard, of the Operetta Theatre, Edinburgh, where she was to have opened on the 25th inst.
17/8/1862

INJUDICIOUS ATTACK by THEATRICALS upon the Press of Liverpool.
PRINCE OF WALES THEATRE. – The engagement of the Nelson Sisters has afforded Mr Henderson his first opportunity of getting into a scrape, and he has not failed to make the best, or rather the worst, of the occasion. Since the Theatre opened, its Manager has been warmly and effectively supported by the local press, and under the fostering care of the Fourth Estate he has become a prosperous and popular man. It was scarcely to be expected, under the circumstances, that he would forget the obligations he has incurred, but such is the case, and we now find Mr Henderson openly defying the Press and daring to question the right of the newspapers to criticise the entertainment he provides. Miss Carry Nelson's acting having elicited a severe but not untruthful critique in one of the local papers, the young lady must needs introduce a vamped Scene into the Burlesque of *Ganem*, wherein she indulges in the coarsest abuse of the unfortunate paper in question. This has been continued every evening during the past

fortnight, and the Theatre during that period has been a scene of unseemly confusion. Miss Nelson plays her part with remarkable *sang froid*, but she commits a fatal error in dealing with an English Press and an English audience as she has been in the habit of dealing with the "roughs" of America and Australia. In this country we regard the stage of a respectable Theatre as a place from which ladies and gentlemen are accustomed to entertain refined and intelligent audiences.

It is with the Manager, however, that we would more particularly remonstrate. In quarreling with the newspapers he is damaging his own reputation, but by mixing up these quarrels with the business of his Theatre, he imposes his personal affairs upon audiences who are presumed to attend his Theatre to witness the pieces advertised for performance. He will speedily discover the error he has committed, as the influence of the Press cannot be damaged by all the Managers in the world. If an unjust criticism should at any time be published, it is not the Manager's or the Actor's province to lampoon the paper in which it appears. The public are the legitimate judges, and to them alone should be left the expression of opinion which the aggrieved party always covets. The day is past for Managers to dictate to Editors, and the Press of this country is too exalted and dignified to tolerate the ridicule of angry Actresses or indiscreet Lessees. The proceedings at this Theatre have hitherto been highly commendable; and, as the Manager appears anxious to merit a continuance of public favour, he will, probably, put an early stop to this "Nelson folly," and desist from his fruitless and dangerous attempt to fetter the Press. Business has not been so good of late, but, as a succession of stars is announced, this Theatre will soon resume its wonted activity.
14/9/1862

TO STRUGGLING TRAGEDIANS. – A LEADING MAN with very little money may have, for £10, a complete Wardrobe – RICHARD, OTHELLO, RICHELIEU, MACBETH, HAMLET, WOLSEY, ROMEO, INGOMAR, GAMESTER, BELPHEGOR, &c., &c., with Boots, Shoes, Sandals, Tights, Paste Buckles, Six Swords, Three Daggers, Macbeth Shield, &c., &c. A useful lot of faded finery, for small Towns. Apply to SAMUEL MAY, 35, BOW STREET, W.C.
19/10/1862

AN ABSCONDING EQUESTRIAN. – At the Cheltenham Police Court on Saturday, before the Chairman, Mr W.M. Skillicome, Esq., and the bench of Magistrates, Emily Guest, aged nineteen, was brought up on a warrant, charged with absconding from the service of her master, Frederick Adolphus Maus, an equestrian, she being his apprentice. It appears that the prisoner had been bound to the prosecutor for a term of seven years, four of which had expired. On the third of the present month she quarrelled with another apprentice when retiring for the night, and bit her on the thigh. For this she was chastised by Mrs Maus, and afterwards walked to Gloucester, where she took a train to Liverpool, and there joined her parents. A warrant was taken out for her apprehension, and she was arrested at Liverpool on Friday by Police-constable Boyd. The case was dismissed on the prisoner promising to return and fulfill her contract.
21/12/1862

4
1863
CLAMBERING UP THE CARYATIDES

WANTED, a SENSIBLE MAN with TWENTY POUNDS. – GRICE, the Wizard, is desirous to meet with a Partner to join him in a Tour through the Provinces. His Apparatus consists of Silver and Glass, Five Tables, with Fringed and Spangled Draperies, Candelabras, &c. Would have no objection to join any respectable concern now travelling. Weight of Apparatus, Boxes included, under One Hundred and Fifty Pounds. Address, 104, High Holborn.
4/1/1863

DASTARDLY OUTRAGE UPON MRS PITT, OF THE THEATRE ROYAL, SHEFFIELD. – On the 1st inst., a very cowardly outrage was inflicted upon Mr Charles Pitt and his family, Mrs Pitt narrowly escaping serious if not fatal injury. Mr Pitt's residence is in Norfolk Street, and on New Year's Eve the family were seated in the drawing-room, waiting the coming-in of the new year. Mrs Pitt appears to have been seated between the gaslight and the window, her shadow consequently being thrown upon the window blind; and while in this position some miscreant deliberately threw a brickbat with great force through the window, striking Mrs Pitt sideways on the back of the head, but fortunately on the dressing of hair, and not on a vital part of the head. No one could be seen in the street, and it is to be feared that there will be no means of bringing the coward who threw the missile to justice, although a reward has been offered for the purpose. The circumstance was alluded to the same night at the Theatre Royal, and prior to the commencement of the pantomime there were cries for Mrs Pitt, who shortly made her appearance on the stage, and was received most flatteringly by a very crowded audience, who testified their sympathy in a very marked manner.

FATAL "BLONDIN" CATASTROPHE. – Gravesend, Jan 10th. - An inquest was held by Mr Hilder, the Borough Coroner, on view of the body of Benjamin Prewett, a man of colour, who died in the Gravesend Infirmary from the effect of a fall from a rope upon which a Female Blondin was performing.
  Robert Abbott, a travelling equestrian, residing at Canterbury, said he had known the deceased four months, and they were attached to a circus belonging to Mace, and they were discharged about eight weeks ago. They consulted together over what they had best do, as witness had a large family, and could not starve. He proposed that he should take the rope in the street and have public performances. They visited Northfleet, and erected a rope across the green. There were six poles to support the rope, which was secured to stakes fixed in the ground. His daughter had performed on the tight-rope for the last two years. The performance took place at three o'clock on the afternoon of Tuesday. She was attired in a Garibaldian dress, and went along the rope the first time safely. The second time she attempted to walk across the rope she had a handkerchief tied over her eyes and a sack placed over her head. She had

reached about the middle of the rope when the deceased climbed up the poles to stand on the rope, so as to receive the performer when she had got to the end of the rope. The deceased called to her to go back, and immediately there was a crash, occasioned by one of the poles breaking, and his daughter and the deceased fell from the rope. He caught his daughter by the waist as she was falling, but she was hurt. The deceased fell to the ground and sustained severe injuries. He was known as Ben Aston, the African Champion. The accident was occasioned by the deceased climbing up the poles, which were not sufficiently strong to bear him.

Henry Lee, who assisted to fix the rope, said the poles were 28ft. long, and the rope 24ft. from the ground. The female on the rope was blindfolded and had a sack on her head.

Mr Gramshaw, surgeon, said the deceased had sustained a fractured arm, injuries to right hip and back and lungs, arising from the fall. He died on Thursday.

The Coroner having summed up, and remarked upon such exhibitions, the jury returned a verdict of accidental death, and strongly condemned the practice of allowing females to ascend ropes placed at so great an altitude, especially in the public streets.

Abbott said his daughter had walked along a rope over the Severn 80ft. high, but he would bear in mind the recommendation of the jury.
11/1/1863

The LAMENTABLE OCCURRENCE at the Princess's Theatre. – The Inquest. – (Yesterday.)
LAST evening Dr Lankester, the Coroner for Central Middlesex, held a long inquiry into the circumstances connected with the death of Sarah Smith, one of the unfortunate sufferers by the melancholy accident which happened at the Princess's Theatre on Friday night, the 23rd ult. The Jury having viewed the body, the appearance of which we spare the harrowing details, the following evidence was adduced: –

Sarah Gibson said – I live at 45, Oakley Street, Lambeth, and am the mother of the deceased. She was seventeen years of age last December. She was employed in what is called the extra ballet at the Princess's Theatre, but was engaged for the whole of the pantomime. She was burned at the Theatre last Friday week. I saw her at the hospital at nine o'clock. She did not tell me how the accident occurred. She was quite sensible, and only said she was very much burnt. She told me that if there were rugs there she could have been saved.

Coroner – Do you impute blame to anyone? Witness – I do not think so because I know nothing about it. […]

Mr Edward Morgan, M.R.C.S., said – I am house surgeon at the Middlesex Hospital. I saw deceased when she was admitted on Friday week, about half past eleven o'clock. She was in a state of collapse at the time, with very extensive burns of the face, neck, temple, back of the upper part of the chest, thighs, both arms, and other parts. One third of the surface of the body was burnt. She never rallied, and sank last Wednesday, dying at a quarter before six in the evening. The cause of the death was exhaustion produced by the burns. There was no internal inflammation. I have since made a *post-mortem* examination, and there was considerable congestion of the internal viscera. She said nothing to me of the cause of the accident.

William Harris – I am super-master at the Princess's Theatre. I engage the extra ballet. Mr Milano engages the ballet. Miss Gibson was in the extra ballet. I was on stage on the night of the accident. It happened on the prompt side – that is, the left side from the audience. I was standing on the other side – the O.P. side. I saw Miss Hunt's clothes and one of the extra ballet in flames on the opposite side. She passed quickly down to the first entrance on that side, and passed a Miss White, who escaped, and in passing Miss Gibson, or Smith, set fire to her. Mr Roxby followed Miss Hunt, threw her down, and with his Inverness cape extinguished the flames.

Coroner – You ran over? Witness – Yes, all of us did.

Coroner – What then? Witness – he returned to Miss Smith, the flames about whom were extinguished by the men about her. Several of them called to her to fall down, but she would not do so. She ran about. She wore more skirts than was usual. She prided herself very much on her appearance. The outside skirt is supplied by the Management.

That was the part that took fire? – Witness – Yes.

Coroner – Have you ever had any inquiries made as to the providing of uninflammable material for the skirts? – Witness – I believe they have been so provided, but you must understand that new dresses were supplied last Monday, and as the solution in which they were dipped only lasts a week or two, even if those they had were so dipped the good effects would have passed off, as they had been in use since the 26th of December last.

By the Coroner – Were the dresses ever washed? Witness – No, never.

Coroner – Then you account for their taking fire that the uninflammable quality had worn out? – Witness – I believe so.

By the Jury – what arrangements are made for extinguishing fire if it should happen? – Witness – I cannot tell you that. I am not the Stage-Manager.

Mr Robert Roxby, who wore his arm in a sling, and appeared otherwise to have suffered from the effects of the fire, said – I am the Stage-Manager at the Princess's. On the evening in question, I saw a person run through the wings, and I rushed at her, and seized her in my arms. She ran in at the front wing on the prompt-side. I seized hold of her clothes and tore them all off, as much as I could, wrapping my Inverness cape round her, and ultimately extinguished the flames. I then saw the deceased in flames, and ran to her, taking off my under coat to extinguish the fire on her.

By the Jury – Have you any means for extinguishing fire? – Witness – We have the hose there, and the two wingmen are supposed to be ready for any emergency, but I do think that it would be advisable to have damp cloths or rugs. In this case it would not have been of any avail. The difficulty I have have always found is to catch the person who is on fire.

Ada Edson, living at No. 1, William Street, Kennington Park, deposed as follows: – I am one of the extra ballet at the Princess's. On Wednesday, January the 23rd, I was standing next to and saw Miss Hunt in flames. I said, "Annie, you are on fire," and she rushed down to the first entrance. I screamed and ran away. I did not see Miss Smith catch fire. I think Miss Hunt caught fire at the tin plates. I do not think the gas could have set light to her. The tin plates were called light-pans. I saw nothing after that, as I ran to the back of the stage. We provide the underskirts, but the management finds the outside tarlatane. I have never tried if they are inflammable or not. Miss Hoggins supplies the skirts. When I saw Miss Hunt on fire it was the blue drapery or mantle that was in flames. The flame was from her waist to her shoulders when I saw it. The drapery is supplied with the tarlatane skirt.

By the Jury – We are not near the gas lights. There is quite sufficient care taken to prevent fire.

Coroner – I may say that I have seen the Theatre lighted up, and there is quite sufficient care taken against the gas. What might be done if any gas escaped I do not know.

William Randle – I am the artist in fireworks to the Princess's Theatre and supply the lights which are used. I make the coloured lights which are used for the purpose of producing the illuminating effects in the Theatre. There were eight burning at the time of the accident on Friday week, four on the prompt side and four on the other. It was a red light that must have burnt these young ladies. I was attending the first light at the second entrance. There was no light at the first entrance. I lighted my light, which changed from green to red. We do it with a wax taper. They are red and green, but do not throw any flame. They contain sulphur, charcoal, nitrate of birita, and nitrate of strontion. There is no gunpowder. (One of the lights was here produced.) They throw out no sparks, but sometimes the fuze will sputter. I use sublime sulphur. The quick match is made with gunpowder and cotton, the powder being worked into a paste, and the cotton rubbed in it. I did not see the accident. I saw Miss Hunt pass me in flames. I did not see any spark from my match, or anyone else's, set fire to Miss Hunt's dress. I have used the lights for thirty years, and never knew an accident to occur before. I knew it could not have happened from the gas, and the probable theory is that the ignition was caused by a spark from the fire-pan. I have, since the accident, thought it might have occurred from the fuze, and I have since introduced another plan of lighting the fire with a Vesuvian light, from which there can be no spark emitted. [...]

The Coroner then summed up, and pointed out that while the actual cause of the calamity, whether by fire-pan or by the igniting cotton, was not clearly ascertained, there was no blame attributable to anyone, and there verdict would therefore be one of "Accidental Death." At the same time they might consider whether some means might not be adopted either to render the dresses uninflammable, of that Managers of Theatres should take such precautions as would prevent, to a vast extent, the repetition of such calamities. He then at some length recapitulated the opinion he had already expressed, and which had been so thoroughly endorsed by the public press and the well-thinking portion of the community of the people, as to the absurdity of the exceeding size of ladies' dresses*, and the Jury returned the following verdict: –

"That on the 28th of January, Sarah Gibson, otherwise Smith, was found dead, and did die from the mortal effects of exhaustion from severe and extensive burns on her body, and the said Jurors further say that the said burns were produced by her clothes taking fire at the Princess's Theatre, and the said Jurors further say that the said death arose from accidental causes."

To this verdict the Jury appended the following recommendation: –

"The Jury wish further to express their opinion that sufficient precautions were not taken at the Princess's Theatre to extinguish any accidental fire taking place in the *corps de ballet*, and they also consider it necessary to urge the necessity of rendering articles of linen and cotton clothing uninflammable."

The inquiry then terminated.

We are happy to be able to add that Mr Morgan, the house surgeon at the hospital, has pronounced Miss Hunt out of danger, a circumstance that will give great satisfaction under the circumstances of this most melancholy affair.

A reference to the fashion for wearing crinolines, which easily caught fire or became caught in machinery.

1/2/1863

MR EDITOR, – Allow me, Sir, through the medium of your widely-circulated paper, to guard visitors to the pantomimes against a novel mode of having their pockets lightened. On Monday afternoon last I went with my little child and a lady to the Princess's Theatre, and upon coming out of the hall, within a few yards of the entrance, a decently-dressed female (who had been in the crowd before me some little time) suddenly turned round and tried to return to the Theatre by pressing between the child and myself. I urged her to pass on the other side of me, but she apathetically remarked, "I want my children," and at the same instant I felt her hand in my pocket. I charged her with it, but knowing that my purse could not have been taken (as I had tied it in my pocket, having lost one on a former occasion), and having no gentleman with me, I allowed her to escape. Hoping you will pardon me for thus troubling you. I remain, Sir, yours respectfully, WIDE-AWAKE.

8/2/1863

TO THE EDITOR OF THE ERA.

Sir, – Will you be so obliging as to allow me a little space for the purpose of calling attention to a subject which, although not one of any great importance, may be classed among the many minor annoyances to which the public are occasionally exposed. I allude to the absurd practice of reading poems in a building like the Crystal Palace to an assemblage of 13,000 persons.

That Mr Phelps is an excellent reader, possessing both skill and power, we all know, but we also know that the human voice has its limits, and all efforts to force it beyond them must fail, and I feel assured that I shall not be charged with exaggeration when I say that out of the 13,000 persons present on

Friday last, 10,000 could not hear a word he was saying. It is true they could see that a recitation was going on in the distance, but that is all they knew of the matter, so that each of this large majority

Sat, like Patience on a monument,
Smiling at Grief.

Such a failure is anything but amusing. A similar thing occurred at the Schiller Festival. On that occasion Dr Kinkel (a good orator with a capital voice) tried to make himself heard by 14,000 people, with similar success to that of Friday. Such an attempt is like a man preaching on the top of St Paul's to a congregation on Bow Common. I have the honour to be, Sir, Your most obedient servant, G.E. May 5th, 1863.
10/5/1863

ON Tuesday afternoon a professional acrobat, named Charles Marsh, accompanied by a friend named Wharton, both of whom were engaged in a singing saloon in Yarmouth, went up the Nelson Monument, erected on the Downs, for the purpose of obtaining a view from the top. When they reached the platform near the summit, Marsh got outside, and succeeded in clambering up the caryatides, and from thence to the image of Britannia, which stands nearly fourteen feet high at the summit. On the image he mounted to the helmet and began to perform there some of his gambols, in the course of which he missed his hold and fell headlong from the trident to the ground, a distance of 140 feet, and was of course killed on the spot. His companion had not seen him go on the top outside, and supposing he had descended the steps within by way of a joke, hastened down to overtake him; but when he arrived at the bottom he found the lifeless body of his friend on the footpath. The accident was witnessed by several spectators on the Downs. The deceased was about thirty-six years of age, and has left a wife and family to mourn the effects of his foolhardiness.

PIANIST. – ENGAGEMENT WANTED by a Young Married Lady, English; a Fine Pianist, of the Royal Academy, whose Husband, a Pole by birth, has deserted her and infant to join in the Polish cause*, leaving her entirely without means. He left home on April 28th, saying that he would return to dinner, but, instead of returning, sailed for Poland, leaving me entirely unprovided for. Wishes for an Engagement in some Entertainment or Exhibition. Address, ELIZABETH WISIGER WALEWSKI, 74, Charlotte Street, Fitzroy Square.
*The January Uprising of 1863 was triggered by the refusal of young Poles to be conscripted into the Imperial Russian Army.
31/5/1863

AT the Hull Police Court on Monday an actor, named James Clifford, who had lately been under an engagement with the Proprietor of a portable Theatre, was placed at the bar, charged with attempting to commit suicide. On Sunday last the prisoner was observed to jump into the Humber Dock Basin, in the presence of a large concourse of spectators, who were witnessing the arrival of some steamers at the pier-head. Attempts were at once made to save the drowning man, and in a short time he was rescued in an exhausted state. Upon being landed on the quay, in a very shivering condition, it was perceived that he was in a destitute state, and wanting food. In answer to the Magistrate, the prisoner said the reason why he wanted to put an end to his life was because he had lost all his theatrical properties, and, being unable to restore them, he found it impossible to obtain another engagement. Having no money, friends, or means of obtaining employment, he was reduced to the necessity of sleeping under the dock-sheds, and seeing no hopes of retrieving his lost position, he determined to rid himself of so burthensome an existence. Several gentlemen in the court offering to assist the poor fellow, the Magistrate released him from custody.
13/9/1863

RIMMEL'S PERFUMED ALMANACK. – The name of this prince of perfumers is too universally known to require at our hands any special recognition; everybody has heard the name of Rimmel, not only from his lavish and gratuitous display of perfume at his fountains at the National Exhibition and the Crystal Palace, but from his perfumed trees and the exquisite odours which are always to be seen and enjoyed in his place of business in the Strand. The elegant little trifle that now calls for our attention to Mr Rimmel, and which bears the above title, is a delicately but richly-perfumed card, which, shutting up like a miniature screen, presents us, on four of its surfaces, with pictorial representations of England, France, Spain, and Russia, each giving us a coloured picture in small of the national sports or pastimes of the different states, a very neat and clever almanack filling up the back of the doubled card. A more elegant or acceptable gift to a lady, to be carried in some mysterious fold of her dress, or else to lie in her writing-desk, we have seldom before seen, and in this belief we fully recommend it to the notice of the public.

ALTERING THEATRICAL TICKETS. – Mr William Miller, Licensed Victualler, Duke's Head, Putney, was brought last Tuesday before Mr Corrie, at Bow Street Police Court, under the following circumstances: – Mr Frederick Balsir Chatterton, joint manager with Edward Falconer of the Theatre Royal, Drury Lane, stated that shortly after seven o'clock on Monday evening the defendant came to him and said he had orders for two, and that he wanted to know why they were not admitted. The witness, on looking at the orders, saw that they had been given to persons for exhibiting the bills of the theatre. They had been originally issued for "Monday, November 2," that date having been written in the handwriting of the clerk, but a figure "3" had since been added, so as to make the date appear to be "Monday, November 23." The witness told the prisoner that it was a benefit night, when the management had no power to give the privilege of admission to any person whatever. The defendant then said he should not leave the theatre, and commenced making a disturbance. The witness remonstrated with him, and begged him to go away quietly, but he continued to make a noise until witness found it necessary to go for a policeman. The witness again begged the defendant to go away quietly, but and on his continued refusal gave him in custody for creating a disturbance in the theatre. Other witnesses confirmed this evidence. The defendant said he was not aware that the orders had been altered. They had been given to him by a friend, now present, who had been equally deceived. Any warmth of temper was owing to the natural indignation he felt at the admission being refused. Mr Clark, a commercial traveller, stated that he had given the orders to Mr Miller. He had received them from a person whose name he mentioned. Mr Corrie remarked that Mr Chatterton was justified in the course he had taken, but it was clear there was a mistake. Mr Miller was discharged, and was perfectly free from any imputation.

FATAL CROWDING AT THE CITY OF LONDON THEATRE. – On Wednesday afternoon Mr H Raffles Walthew, the Deputy Coroner for Middlesex, held an inquest at the Duke of Northumberland Tavern, Worship Street, Shoreditch, respecting the death of John Williamson, aged sixteen years, a shoeblack, who died in the City of London Theatre on Wednesday, the 18th inst.

Thomas Samuel Stembridge, Moore's Gardens, Long Alley, said that he was on the staircase, and was walking before the deceased, who was trying to get up before other persons, when he got squeezed against one of the doors. There were about forty persons at that part, which was on the second floor, near the money-taker's box. The deceased began to cry, and could hardly catch his breath. Witness exclaimed, "Jack, go and sit up in that corner." The deceased did not go upstairs, and witness believed that the deceased was suffocated by the heat of the crowd. Witness went for Mr Allinson, the surgeon, who examined deceased, and pronounced life extinct. Did not see anyone use violence against deceased, excepting in the "crush" of the crowd near the door, at the top of the stairs.

Thomas Caslake, 16, Waterloo Place, High Street, Newington, stated that he was check-taker at the gallery of the City of London Theatre, and on the evening in question witness saw deceased scrambling up the stairs between the money-paying place and the check-box. Witness advised deceased to come up and get the benefit of the air, as there was a large window open. Deceased said that he was ill, and appeared in great pain. Witness called the Police Sergeant, who took the deceased out of the way. A glass of ginger-beer was given to him, but deceased could not swallow it. The rush of persons was not so great as witness had seen before, and there had never been an accident in the Theatre before.

Mr John Allinson, M.R.C.S., of Norton Felgate, said that he found deceased quite dead, with livid countenance, and frothy mucus issuing from his mouth. There were no external marks of violence. The deceased had died from congestion of the lungs, caused by excitement, consequent on a pressure from the crowd, as he (deceased) was suffering at the time from disease of the heart.

Mr Edward Waller, the Summoning Officer, said that the Theatre had only been open a few minutes, and it was impossible to keep boys from rushing into the crowd. The Theatre was one of the best conducted in the Metropolis. The Jury returned a verdict "That the deceased died from congestion of the lungs consequent from pressure from a crowd at the City of London Theatre, accidentally and by misfortune."
29/11/1863

FIVE THOUSAND PANTOMIME POSTERS Now Ready. Large Assortment of various Grotesque Designs. A separate Picture for every Pantomime. Thus Managers will not be inconvenienced by any other Theatre using the same Pictorial. Sizes from one sheet Double Crown to any size. One Hundred Comic Pictures, Two Feet and a Half by Three Feet Four Inches for One Pound. P.O.O. to Chief Office, GEORGE WARD and COMPANY, Designers, Lithographers, Engravers, and Printers, 3, Snow Hill, London.
27/12/1863

5
1864
A SEVERE BLOW WITH AN UMBRELLA

TO THE EDITOR OF THE ERA.

Sir, – The taste for amateur theatricals is rapidly increasing in this country, and they bid fair to become the most popular amusement of the coming season. That they do good in many ways both to the Theatrical Profession and the world in general there can be no doubt, and they should, therefore, be encouraged as much as possible. But there is one kind of encouragement which is fast becoming an evil. I mean the indiscriminate praise lavished by the Press on all amateurs who (if one is to believe newspaper accounts) are all equal to if not superior to any professional actors.

I grant that in most amateur companies there is one star with a natural talent for acting, which, if properly developed by study, might make him or her a first-rate performer, but for the rest, the most that can be said of them is that *they get through their parts fairly*, and that is generally all they hope to do. Why, then, should I, having, as I say myself, "got through my part fairly," be told in the next paper that "Mr ------'s performance of ------ was one of the most finished pieces of acting it has ever been our lot to witness. Were he on the London boards, Wigan, Robson (or whoever it was I had copied) would have to look to their laurels." I have seen such a paragraph often lately; the system of perpetual praise is carried to even a worse extent with regard to amateur actresses, who, according to the papers, are one and all, without exception, superior to any of those ladies who have made the stage their study and profession for years. Of course there are a few good amateur actresses – one in particular I consider to be the best (in her line) either professional of amateur, since Mrs Keeley, and I have seen a few other good ones; but with the majority, when you have said that they were dressed in perfect taste, and looked very well on the stage, you have given all the praise you fairly can.

I have had the good fortune to attend a great many amateur performances in the past two years, and five times out of six none of the ladies could be heard beyond the first six rows of seats. Yet in most cases the next paper contained a florid account of their beautiful acting and clear bell-like voices.

In all accounts of amateur actors, their efforts should be looked on with a lenient eye; but when good, bad, and indifferent are equally pronounced to be perfect, how are those who really wish to improve to find out where they have failed, and what to try and improve on? No one believes these grandiloquent accounts. Pray, sir, use your influence to have substituted some more impartial criticism, which would be of advantage to amateur actors, and which their friends could depend one. I enclose my card, and am, Sir, your most obedient servant, AN AMATEUR. Feb. 14th, 1864.

21/2/1864

WANTED, a NEWFOUNDLAND DOG; one that can work Stage Business. Colour, Black and White preferred. Wanted at once. State price and particulars to A.B., care of Mr Bradley, 41, Chariot Street, Hull.
6/3/1864

TO THE EDITOR OF THE ERA.
Sir, – In an admirable letter which appeared in the pages of *Punch* a week or two since, we find this question asked: "What becomes of our Columbines, our fairies, and our sylphs when they are over fifty, or are weakened in their legs?" *What, indeed!* The ladies of the ballet have no fund at which to apply for relief in sickness or old age, and their scanty salaries preclude the possibility of their laying by anything against a rainy day. Now, Sir, I feel convinced that if the influence of *The Era* were brought to bear in this matter, a plan might be devised for organising a fund in aid of the cause, and once organised, I happen to know there are many who would gladly come forward and subscribe thereto. If half the people who are charmed with the "Realms of Rapture" and "Bowers of Bliss" at Christmas time (to the success of which the ballet so largely contribute) were to contribute their mite according to their means, it would form a considerable sum to start with. As the writer in *Punch* observes, "If the ballet girls be needful to the pleasure of society, I think society might stretch a hand to help them in their need." No one would be better pleased to see this accomplished than yours truly, FOOTLIGHT.

[Our correspondent will be glad to be informed, and our contemporary will not be vexed to be corrected respecting the subject which they have both taken up with so much kind feeling. The General Theatrical Fund admits all Pantomimists, as well as performers generally, to participate in the privileges accorded to subscribers, and the Dramatic, Equestrian, and Musical Sick Fund is available for all dancers in the hour of their need. If the many so happily known to "Footlight" will now come forward and contribute to increase the funds at the disposal of both these useful Institutions, they will have the best opportunity of carrying out their object in the best manner. Perhaps "Footlight" and his friends will accept an invitation to dinner at the Freemasons' Tavern for next Thursday at six o'clock. By the kind permission of Mr Buckstone, they will be allowed to bring their cheque-books with them. ED. of ERA.]
20/3/1864

WANTED, a SMALL DWARF WOMAN, or a TALL GIANT, to exhibit with a Dwarf Man. Apply to C. PAWTREES, 24, Calvert Street, Shoreditch.
3/4/1864

ASSAULTING A CIRCUS PERFORMER. – Mr Richard Hayes, of the circus establishment, Market Square, Bolton, was brought before the Borough Magistrates, on Saturday morning, under a warrant charging him with assaulting a young girl under twelve years of age, named Selina Hickey. It appears that the young girl and her brother, who are orphan children, are apprenticed with Messrs Hayes to the equestrian art. On the previous evening the girl was delayed on her entry into the first "act," which gave rise to a display of bad feeling on the part of defendant, who struck her a severe blow on the left temple with an umbrella, inflicting a wound from which blood streamed freely. In that condition she went to the police office, accompanied by her aunt, and these proceedings were taken. Application was also made to quash the indentures. Defendant agreed to cancel the agreement, and Mr Hall, solicitor, drew up an undertaking to that effect, but Hayes afterwards declined to sign it. For the assault the Magistrates inflicted a penalty of 20s. and costs, and further proceedings will be taken to quash the indentures.
15/5/1864

TO THE EDITOR OF THE ERA.
Sir, – You will greatly oblige by giving the following publication in your valuable paper: – In your publication of the 8th there appeared an advertisement for a "Lady Vocalist in any line," I answered the same, and received an engagement from the advertiser, J. M------, not a hundred miles from Burnley, for

one month, half my fare to be paid when I arrived, and the other half when I wished to return, the advertiser informing me, by letter, that it was a respectable house, and that he had had several ladies from London, who had always been respected; but when I arrived, after a journey of 250 miles, he refused to pay my half fare, and I found that I had been enticed all the way from London to a place with no licence, and the worst night house in the town. Alone, and nearly dead with fright, caused by what I was compelled to witness, and should have had to submit to if I had stopped in such a den of crime, I left the house as soon as I could get a chance, and was obliged to walk about a strange town without money, and not knowing where to go or what to do till I went to inquire for my box of the station master, to whom I related my circumstance, and who took me to the house of a Mr G------, where I was received with great kindness, and was told that I was the third female that had been served in the same way, and that I was very fortunate in getting away, as the last young lady they kept locked up for a week. J. M------ refused to pay me for my expenses and trouble, and I have been obliged to return to town, after having refused three engagements to go to the above. Perhaps the publication of this may serve as a warning to others, as it has done to me. I am, Sir, yours obediently, CATHERINE W. May 20th 1864.

WANTED, for the ROYAL NAVY, for a Ship in the Pacific, a YOUNG MAN that can Play the Harmonium, and can Teach Boys to Sing in Church. All Expenses will be paid to the Ship. An excellent opportunity of seeing the world. For Particulars, apply to Mr JOHN CONSTABLE, 10, Berkeley Street, Southsea, Portsmouth. A Few Clarionet Players Wanted for the Channel Fleet.
29/5/1864

TO THE EDITOR OF THE ERA.
Dear Sir, – Believing that I am the party referred to in the letter signed "Catherine W.," which appeared in your publication of Saturday last, I take the earliest opportunity to reply to it. I did advertise in *The Era* for a female vocalist. The lady who was engaged by that means, on her arrival at my house in Burnley, I found to be far advanced in a state of pregnancy. On ascertaining her vocal abilities, I was astonished to find her utterly unfit for me, even at her engaged salary of 25s. per week. Previous to her arrival I was favoured with what purported to be her *carte-de-visite*, but when I saw what should have been the original, I found I had been imposed upon. A short conversation convinced me that matters of a purely domestic nature caused her to be fretful and uneasy away from home. She was continually talking about her husband, who she said had several young persons engaged in crinoline work. That my house is a "den of crime" is a libel and a falsehood. It is closed every evening, in accordance with the terms of my licence, punctually at eleven o'clock. That a person was "ever locked up in my house for a week" is another falsehood. I have kept my present Concert Room for six years, during which time I have paid upwards of £3,000 to the Profession. Are provincial proprietors of Concert Saloons to be victimised by *soi-distant* professionals, who invariably hail from the Metropolis? Instead of Catherine W. being the sufferer, I am the sufferer, inasmuch as I lost the services of a very talented artiste through the disappointment caused by her. As to my treatment of professionals, the subjoined certificate speaks for itself: –

"We, the undersigned, hereby certified that we have been treated in every respect by Mr John Mosedale as consonant with his duty to our profession and engagements. – Wat Melton, comic vocalist; Mary Melton, sentimental; W. Beeson, pianist (eighteen months' engagement); Alice Wilson, serio-comic; W. Hayley, descriptive."

Your insertion of the above will oblige yours truly, JOHN MOSEDALE. Burnley, June 1st, 1864.
5/6/1864

AT an inquest, held on Wednesday last at the Royal Hotel in Westfield Street, St Helen's, on view of the body of Robert Stoddart, the celebrated comedian, performing with the well-known Family of

"Stoddarts," who met with his death under the following circumstances. On the previous Saturday night, in consequence of a rush at the doors of the Theatre before the time of opening, the deceased voluntarily undertook to open the doors, and as there was no other road only from the stage, he missed his footing in stepping across from the proscenium to the orchestra, and fell with all his weight against the outside rail, rupturing his liver. He plucked up in the best way he could, and performed his part of Eelskin Jack, in *The Poor Girl's Temptation*, until nearly the conclusion of the second scene, when his brother Richard, finding that he was struggling against intensity of pain from injuries received, sent him home in a cab. He was immediately attended by Dr Twyford's assistant, but his effort and skill were unavailing. He died at half-past one on Monday morning. A verdict of "Accidental death" was returned. The deceased was thirty-five years of age.
27/7/1864

MR EDITOR. – Sir, – Knowing your paper to be the principal medium for entertainments, I wish to say a few words that respectable ones may not be prevented from visiting our city of Bedford. On Friday last one arrived under the title of "Kalsall's Waxworks," and built in the Market Place. But the continual annoyance to the tradesmen with two drums, cymbals, and gong going from two o'clock until midnight is rather too much, keeping the tradesmen's families around awake two hours after their usual time. If you will kindly insert this it may be a caution to others, or I think it most likely all entertainment will be stopped coming into the best situation in the city. I am, Sir, yours respectfully, ONE OF THE TWENTY TRADESMEN ROUND THE MARKET PLACE WHO OBJECTED TO IT. Bedford, August 1st, 1864.
7/8/1864

AT half past eight last (Friday) evening, during the performance of *The Woman of Business*, and while Mr Phillips, Mr J.L. Toole, and Mr Stephenson were on the stage, a sudden panic ran through the audience, owing to cries of "Fire!" from persons in the gallery, and the audience suddenly rose with a view to rush out of the house, although they were assured by the police on duty at the Theatre, and Mr Stephenson and Mr Phillips, that there was no cause for alarm, that no fire existed in any part of the theatre, and that the smoke which had caused the alarm arose from a wood fire in the chimney of an adjoining baker's, which had penetrated through one of the open windows. Unfortunately, the alarm spread outside that the Theatre was on fire, and engines from the Chandos and Farringdon stations arrived, adding to the unnecessary consternation. The firemen were refused admission, it being considered that their appearance would cause a second panic. The audience, being at length satisfied, resumed their seats, and the performances were continued. One gentleman had his shoulder dislocated.
11/9/1864

MR EDITOR. – Sir, on Friday evening last I had announced an entertainment at the Temperance Hall here, which was to include the "Ghost" illusion. My wife procured the chemicals required for making oxygen gas for the "lime light" at the shop of Messrs Nichol and Ord, High Street. I placed them in a retort as usual, and having left them for a moment they exploded, doing considerable damage to the room in which they were placed, and severely burning two females who were present. The unaccountable nature of this explosion caused me to examine the remainder of the chemicals, and I found Mrs M. had been served with "Black Antimony" instead of Black Oxide of Manganese. The remainder of the materials used were taken possession of by the Trustees of the building, and are now in their hands, and there is no mistake about the explosion being caused by the sulphur in the "Black Antimony," and the Chlorate of Potash. I trust you will give these few lines a place in your columns, as explaining what would otherwise seem rather unaccountable. Your obedient servant, EDWIN MORLEY. Hartlepool, 21st September.
25/9/1864

THE ROPE-TYING MANIA.
HERR TOLMAQUE AT ST MARTIN'S HALL. – On Wednesday evening last, Herr Tolmaque, who claims to be the original performer of the "rope trick" in England, gave a "complimentary *soiree* to his friends." The sole object of this *séance* was to expose the spiritual "swindle," as the lecturer terms it; and to prove that the escape from any elaborate system of knotted bonds is perfectly easy of attainment without the aid of emissaries from the other world. A large proportion of the audience were manifestly of Herr Tolmaque's opinion concerning the absurd pretensions of the ghostly Brothers Davenport*, which unanimity of sentiment made it the more remarkable that such irregularity should have pervaded the social atmosphere of St Martin's Hall. Herr Tolmaque came forward in a good cause, and to prove his own assertion. His success was eventually acknowledged by long-continued applause, on his liberating himself from what appeared to be the most absolute restraint.

After a few tricks of ordinary legerdemain, the real business of the evening commenced. The appeal for some member of the audience to secure the ropes around Herr Tolmaque produced a variety of vociferous suggestions, which ended in Captain Burton, the celebrated explorer, undertaking that duty. From what we could gather from the confusion prevailing among the audience, Captain Burton was objected to by Herr Tolmaque, from having hinted at the necessity for a partial stoppage of circulation. This point was argued at some length, and subsequently Captain Burton left the platform. Doctor Hawkins undertook the duty of securing the lecturer, who was then enclosed in a "structure," and almost immediately put his hand through openings cut in the screen. The front was removed, and Herr Tolmaque walked forward perfectly free. A more severe test was next submitted to. Dr Izard and Dr Frank Buckland (who, in the estimation of the audience, were evidently adepts in the art of knot-tying), bound Herr Tolmaque, hand and foot, to the chair, in a most ingenious manner. This operation was eight minutes in being completed. A tambourine, guitar, and bell, were then shut up in the structure with the lecturer, and in a wonderfully short space of time the tambourine was thrown out among the persons near the stage; the real hands and some cadaverous imitations appeared through the openings; the guitar was sounded and the bell rung. Herr Tolmaque had again released himself, and was greeted with the most enthusiastic demonstrations of approval. He then reversed the order of things, and, shut up in the structure, bound himself to the chair, offering five hundred pounds to the individual who could untie the knots. This was, of course, impossible, as he held the ends of the ropes in his hands, and thus one trick *pur et simple* was candidly explained. Herr Tolmaque concluded with a few remarks, or rather a string of invectives, against the fraternal delusions of Hanover Square, and disappeared uttering the very forcible and appropriate speech of Emilia in Othello:

Oh Heaven! That such companions thou'dst unfold,
And put in every honest hand a whip,
To lash the rascals naked through the world.

The gas was not turned down during any period of the *séance*. At the Eccleston Square *soiree*, in which Herr Tolmaque performed, the musical instruments are asserted to have been seen "flying about the room," which was not in darkness, but illuminated by oil lamps. It is but fair to say that this manifestation did not take place on Wednesday.
The Davenport Brothers were American performers who claimed that their feats of escapology, performed inside a closed cabinet, were accomplished with the aid of spirits.
6/11/1864

MR EDITOR. – Sir, as the organ of theatrical matters and the staunch friend of the Profession generally, permit me to ask you to expose the following: – On three or four occasions, being in want of members to complete my company, I have inserted advertisements in your valuable paper, and received many applications in reply; some of these parties, by pleading poverty to take a journey, have induced me to send them money to do so, and within the last two months three parties have had money sent (10s., 15s.,

and 18s.); and, with the exception of one (who returned the post-office order for 10s.), I have neither seen the people nor the money; and, last week, to complete it, a married man, with wife, engaged, and wrote to me to send them £1, which I did. I now learn that with my money they have gone to another situation, not only deceiving me by not coming, with their names announced in my bills, and causing serious disappointment, but cheating me of my hard-earned money, which I can ill afford to lose, and compelling me to advertise for others, for whom I must at great inconvenience wait. Surely, Sir, this state of things ought not to be allowed, and I do not doubt others have been served the same way. Apologising for troubling you with such an epistle, I beg to subscribe myself, honoured Sir, your obedient servant and subscriber, WILLIAM MONTAGUE, Theatre Royal, Hastings.
11/12/1864

Sewing Machine for Mrs General Tom Thumb.
THE popular and petite Mrs Stratton's time has been, and is likely to be, fully occupied during her stay in Europe. Inquisitive sight-seers are the last people in the world who would be satisfied to let the General's charming little wife sit, like another Penelope, and keep her multitudinous admirers at bay with any kind of needlework. Under these circumstances, the domestic blessing just completed for Mrs Stratton's enjoyment by Messrs Wheeler and Wilson, the celebrated sewing machine-makers of 139, Regent Street, will possess its full value on the little lady's return to America, and private life. The machine is called, from its dimensions, the "Fairy," and is, in fact, a working model, constructed with the greatest care, and every part of finished workmanship. It is in all particulars well adapted for Mrs Stratton's use, as an ordinary one would be for a more commonplace, or more common-sized mortal. The body of the case is of rosewood, richly carved and inlaid with patterns formed in pearl and gold. The entire case is twenty inches in height, and fifteen in depth, besides being lined throughout with satin wood. The metal wheels, shafts, &c., are gilt plated. Appropriate subjects are painted on the panels, and are as follows: – Cupid and Psyche, the wedding in Grace Church, the bridal drive in Central Park, the General as "Young America," Mrs Stratton as Columbia, a representation of hand sewing and machine work, and round the top, a pattern formed of the American coat of arms, and cherubs after Raphael.
18/12/1864

DONATO. – This extraordinary *artiste*, with only one leg, who is to make his first appearance at Covent Garden on Boxing Night, is, we are given to understand by those who have witnessed his performance, a perfect marvel. Not only does he dance in such a manner as to cause the spectator to doubt his own senses, but his performance on the castanets, and his wonderful *aplomb*, precision, agility, &c., are described as unlike anything of the kind ever seen before. Wherever he has appeared, not only has he caused a perfect *furore*, but literally "drawn the town." One of his principal feats is a shawl or mantle dance, described as "Danse avec Manteau," which he will introduce at Covent Garden Theatre on Monday evening. He was formerly a member of the ballet at the San Carlo Theatre in Naples, where his talents as a dancer were much appreciated. From Naples he went to Spain, where he entered the bull-ring, and while acting as a matador he was gored in the thigh, and had to have his leg amputated. His one-legged dancing, as we have before stated, procured him nothing better than an engagement at a Concert Hall in Lyons, where he was receiving one of those small salaries, counted in francs, which are so common on the continent. Transplanted from Lyons, he made great reputation in Germany.

THE VERY LATEST SENSATION. – THE ONE-LUNG SOPRANO and the WOODEN-LEGGED CONTRALTO, worthy the attention of Operatic, Dramatic, and Music Hall Managers. Their Motto (quite Operatic), "Go It, Yer Cripples."
25/12/1864

6
1865
WHAT JOLLY DOGS ARE WE!

FATAL ACCIDENT AT COVENT GARDEN THEATRE. – On Thursday evening an inquiry was held by Mr Bedford, Westminster Coroner, at the Strand Union Board Room, Bow Street, touching upon the death of James Chamont, aged forty-eight. Matthew Morgan, employed at the Theatre, said that during the performance of the Pantomime of *Cinderella* on Monday afternoon he saw deceased fall through from the middle floor into the cellar beneath.* The witness ran to the cellar, and found him apparently dead. Mr M. Cawood, Secretary to the Covent Garden Company, said the deceased was in the act of putting a board across the trap-door for an actress to stand upon, when he accidentally slipped through. John Garnsey, manager of the machinery in the cellar, said that the deceased's left leg slipped in. he came down with great force upon his back. He never spoke after. He fell about twenty feet. Dr Beale proved that the deceased ruptured the spinal cord, and that death was, of course, instantaneous. After the Coroner and Jury had visited the scene of the occurrence, a verdict of "Accidental death" was returned.
Less than two months later an almost identical accident at this theatre claimed the life of John Walters, a stage carpenter.

A FRIGHTFUL accident took place at Springthorpe's Concert Hall, Dundee, on Monday evening, by which twenty persons were suddenly deprived of life and a number seriously injured. The Hall is situated at the corner of West Bell Street and Constitution Road, underneath Bell Street Church, and below the level of the street, the principal entrance being from Constitution Road by a stair about six feet in breadth and ten in height, secured at the top by a pair of iron gates. Between the foot of the stair and the pay-box is a flagged space, about seven feet long and the same width as the stair, on which, on Monday evening, twenty human beings (men, women, and children), were crushed to death.

Monday being a holiday in Dundee, hundreds of eager pleasure-seekers thronged to "Springthorpe's" popular place of amusement, and congregated in front of the Hall hours before the usual time of opening, over a thousand persons, it is computed, being present at the time of the accident. In order to relieve the pressure outside Mrs Springthorpe resolved to open the Hall an hour sooner, and the usual plan of admission in such cases was adopted, viz., partially opening one gate, so as to admit three or four persons, and then closing it until they had paid and passed into the Hall. This continued until the Hall was about one-third filled, when the pressure became too great for the gate-keeper to withstand. The partly-open gate was forced wide open, a young man in the crowd undid the fastenings of the other, and the living tide swept down the stair (as an eye-witness said) "like a huge black cloud." The foremost were carried off their feet and thrown down at the foot of the stair, those immediately behind falling over and upon them until the bodies were piled to the height of five or six feet.

Those in the Hall, and such as were able among the crowd on the stair, entreated the mob above to stand back, but their entreaties were disregarded by the selfish wretches who were bent on gaining admission, no matter at what cost. Fully *twenty* minutes elapsed ere the stair could be cleared and the gates shut, when the melancholy task of removing the closely-packed bodies was proceeded with. Of these twenty (mostly young people) were either dead when taken up, or expired shortly afterwards. A good many were severely if not fatally injured. A most disgraceful want of feeling was displayed by a number of those who had entered the Hall before the accident, in refusing to leave unless the money was returned. An official inquiry is being made as to the cause of the accident, and the Hall is at present closed.
8/1/1865

Strange Proceedings by Converted Men (Lunatics) in Sheffield.
THE following extraordinary scene we copy from the Sheffield *Daily Telegraph* of last Tuesday, and must express our surprise that the police did not interfere, for the wretched lot appear proper candidates for a lunatic asylum or the station-house: –

Placards having being circulated in the town, stating that Harvey Teasdale, the well-known man monkey and Clown, would relate his "experiences," and destroy his dresses and theatrical effects at the Temperance Hall last night, the place was crowded by persons desirous of witnessing the proceeding. The affair was in connection with what is called "The Hallelujah Band," which is composed of men who state that they have been "converted" from infidelity to religion. The leaders of the band are prize fighters, race runners, "poor miserable wretches," men who have filled the lower walks of comedy, as banjo players and "Niggers." Some of them do not hesitate to state that, before conversion, they had descended into the lowest depths of blackguardism, and one man admitted last night that he had, whilst a sot, "nearly starved to death one of the best little wives that ever breathed." The proceedings are of a decidedly novel description, and give rise to demonstrations of an extraordinary character, such as jumping, shouting, and gesticulations of a most exciting and alarming nature. The service is varied after the style of an ordinary religious service, and consists of singing, prayer, and addresses, the addresses being frequent and boisterous. The "religious melodies," or "ditties," as the hymns are called, are sung to popular airs, and being joined in by some hundreds of voices, lustily exerted, produce a remarkable effect. Last night four or five men conducted the proceedings, and, much to the surprise of those who have only attended ordinary religious services, they took off their coats and unbuttoned their waistcoats, in which condition they stood in a row before the audience. The manner in which they discharged the duties devolving upon them – leading the singing, offering up prayer, and delivering addresses – fully justified the unrobing with which they commenced, their demeanour being for the most part of a violent and exhaustive character. [...]

The feature of the evening was, however, the destruction of the trappings and effects of Harvey Teasdale; and when it was proposed that the congregation should first sing two verses of a melody, there was some hissing, which led to the rebuke, "Now, lads, none of that – remember this is a place of worship." A bundle was at length produced, and it was stated that its contents had long been used in the service of the devil. On being opened a decidedly miscellaneous stock was discovered, and was about to be destroyed, when a slight commotion at the platform door indicated the arrival of an important personage. In another moment a gentleman in his shirt sleeves stepped forward, and announced that Mr Edward Lauri, the Clown at the Surrey Theatre, had just arrived, and that he would be able to state whether the things destroyed were such as would form the wardrobe of a person occupying the position of a Clown and man monkey.

When Lauri stepped forward he was received with a burst of cheering, which he acknowledged in an off-hand and decidedly unconcerned manner, and then took a seat in such a position as he would be able to see the dresses and effects which were about to be sacrificed. Things which had been used in the play of *The Dumb Man of Manchester* and similar pieces were held up and then cut up by the gentlemen in their shirt sleeves, who performed the work of destruction with evident satisfaction, and every now and then varied the monotony of the proceedings by suddenly exclaiming, in the most excited manner, "Hallelujah!" and "Praise the Lord!", "Aye, lad." The dress in which Mr Teasdale performed the character of the Wild Man of the Woods was torn into shreds with the utmost eagerness, and then followed MS. music, manuscript plays, burlesques, and pantomimes, some of which were described as being worth several pounds. Lauri examined all these books and papers previous to their being torn up, and as he did so he was more than once advised by a voice from the gallery to "shuv 'em in his pocket."

As the work of demolition proceeded, Mr Teasdale related anecdotes and circumstances in reference to the articles. "This has gone through many a clock face," holding up what looked like the skin of a poodle dog; "and now it's going through the scissors," said a gentleman in his shirt sleeves, snatching the "effect" and cutting it in two in a twinkling. "Did you ever see a transformation scene like that?" said Mr Teasdale, and then went on to horrify his audience by the relation of a design concocted by a party of Bosjesmen* to take his life, whose hatred he had contracted by some antics he played on them at the Dundee Theatre Royal. The last thing destroyed was the dress which Mr Teasdale used when he appeared as the "man monkey." The dress was stuffed with straw, and its exhibition created much merriment. Two of the gentlemen in their shirt sleeves mounted the table in order to hold the thing up for inspection, and the other gentlemen in their shirt sleeves attacked it with some vigour, one slashing off the tail, and then amputating part of a leg, and so on. When Lauri was about to leave he intimated that the reason he attended was because Mr Teasdale had offered to sell things to him for £2 10s., but now he refused. Lauri also stated that he had been to Leeds that afternoon, and was there informed that Mr Teasdale had already destroyed his effects in that town. This announcement was received with laughter by part of the audience, and Mr Teasdale said, "Aye, you see my enemies are at work."

The meeting was then addressed by a man who gave himself two titles, "Spring-maker Jack, from Cammell's," and also "Jack Birch, the converted banjo player." He described his former life in dark and dismal colours, and shouted till he was hoarse of the happiness which his reformed life afforded him. His disgust with strong drink was most emphatic, and he solemnly declared that he would "rather have a kick from a horse than a swill from a publican." Harvey Teasdale, whose speech was preceded by a "religious melody," followed with an account of his "experiences." They were very much of the same character as the others which had preceded them, and contained revelations, the policy of disclosing which might be very seriously questioned. Altogether the proceedings were of a remarkable and unusual description.

*South African Bushmen.
29/1/1865

TO THE EDITOR OF THE ERA.
Sir, – May I be permitted, through your columns, to say a few words about the subject of encoring at the Theatres? On Tuesday night, at the Olympic, a very vulgar and indifferently executed dance in the Extravaganza was twice encored by the pit, and given therefore three times, to the annoyance of all who were not clever enough to see its extreme merit. I ask, is the pit the only part of the Theatre to be consulted? And even if any part is encored once, is it not preposterous and absurd to give it a third time? Miss Kate Terry showed her good sense and good taste in refusing to appear between the acts of *The Hidden Hand*, though loudly called for; and if all actors and actresses would have the courage to act as she did, there would be less noise in the Theatre and less dissatisfaction among the rest of the audience. I remain, Sir, your obedient servant, A LOVER OF THE THEATRE.
5/3/1865

ONE TRAGEDY INTERRUPTED BY ANOTHER. – On the 17th inst., during the performance of *Othello* in a travelling Royal Prince of Wales Theatre, at Walsall, upon the conclusion of the third act Iago came before the curtain and requested the indulgences of the audience, as an event had occurred which necessitated the temporary cessation of the performance. Before speculation could have proceeded far as to the cause of this abrupt pause in the evening's entertainment, Othello presented himself, and in real and not simulated agitation stated that the nature of the accident which had occurred was such as to render the continuance of the performance of that evening a moral impossibility. One of the lady attendants having been attempted to be defrauded by a little boy who sought access to the Theatre, she, in an impulse of the moment, ran after him, intending to visit him with some mark of her disapprobation, when she was suddenly seized with a spasmodic affliction, it was presumed of the heart, fell down, and immediately expired. The proceeds of the evening would be given to charitable institutions, and he therefore trusted that the audience would quietly and orderly disperse. The Manager then came forward and added his solicitations, deploring the occurrence of an event so melancholy. The audience acquiesced in the request made, and left the Theatre. The deceased was an actress, named Mrs William Howell, thirty years of age. She had for some time been under medical treatment for heart disease at one of the Birmingham hospitals, joined the company on Wednesday, and took part in the performances on Thursday evening. The performance on Friday evening was for the benefit of the Cottage Hospital.

Fire-Proofing Theatres, Dresses, &c.
LAST Saturday afternoon a lecture, illustrated with interesting experiments, was given at the Philharmonic Hall, Islington, on an entirely new and effective method of rendering materials uninflammable, which method has been introduced to the public by Messrs Sylvester and Wilson, the first-named gentleman being the inventor. The lecturer was Mr Dawson, who commenced his discourse by referring to the lamentable catastrophes by fire which so frequently occur, more especially in connection with Theatres and places of amusement generally. [...]

After referring with much pathos to the misery caused by these catastrophes, even when no sacrifice of life occurred, Mr Dawson proceeded to show how, at a merely nominal expense, they might be prevented in future by the invention of Mr Sylvester (who, bye-the-bye, is the proprietor of the splendid illuminated fountain, called the "Minniehaha," at the Philharmonic). The new invention of Mr Sylvester consists in the application of an inflammable material in solution, and which appears to be different to any other previously put forth. The lecturer proceeded to give experiments. He first applied the system to two pieces of common firewood, one of which had been rendered blaze-proof by the new process, whilst the other was in its natural state. The result was that the prepared wood could not be made to burn, and was but slightly charred, whilst the other was quickly burnt in two. Another experiment with a thicker piece of wood, coated with hemp soaked in spirits of wine, was tried with similar results. The lecturer then showed how the system might be applied not only to theatrical dresses, but also to dresses of ladies in private life, and thus an end be put to the dreadful crinoline fatalities, which carry painful distress to so many homes. A lay figure, with distended dress, was consumed in a minute; whilst the dress of a lady, in *propria persona*, was attempted to be set alight in vain. Next an ordinary muslin curtain was set ablaze, whilst another, to which the fire-proofing process had been applied, was but slightly discoloured when a light was placed beneath it. The process could be applied to a dress at a cost of one penny, whilst a large number could be done for even a farthing each. Experiments were then shown on periodicals with a like result, the lecturer referring meanwhile to the practice of reading in bed. One great advantage of the system was that the fabric of dresses was not injured at all by it. A bundle of hay was rendered uninflammable by the process, which can be applied on a more extensive scale so as to adapt it to farm produce and buildings; an advantage, too, of the invention is that hay or other provender is not rendered injurious, so that it may be eaten by cattle with impunity.

The lecturer, who was loudly applauded, concluded by stating that illustrations of this invention would be given in other parts of London; and we doubt not that the subject will receive the attention which it certainly deserves, even if the invention be regarded simply in the light of a means for retarding the progress of flame. Meanwhile communications on the subject may be addressed to Messrs Sylvester and Wilson, 173, St John Street Road, Clerkenwell.
26/3/1865

SENSATION ADVERTISING! – The modern Managerial fashion of bringing out announcements in front of the Theatres to inform the public of the state of the house was neatly parodied in a northern commercial town. A short time ago, when Mr Howard Paul was giving his entertainments at a rival establishment in the same town, the Theatre was doing a notoriously bad business; but the Manager, true to his tactics of impressing the outside public, continued his plan of hanging out placards – "PIT FULL," "ONLY STANDING ROOM IN THE BOXES," when it was a well-known fact that the Theatre was almost empty. This doubtful policy forming the subject of a good deal of local gossip, Mr Howard Paul, by way of a practical joke, had a burlesque set of placards in the same type and style painted, and at six o'clock in the evening, before the doors were open, a huge bill appeared in the front of the Hall, "VERY EMPTY." A little later the public were informed that there were "TWO IN THE PIT." This was removed to make way for one still larger and more imposing, "SUFFICIENT IN TO FORM AN AUDIENCE." At nine o'clock another loomed out, "ROOM TO LIE FULL LENGTH IN ANY PART OF THE HOUSE," and when the entertainment was over, and the audience departed, "NOT A SOUL IN YET FOR TOMORROW NIGHT'S PERFORMANCE." This travestie of *les affiches* caused immense amusement in the town, and the placard-loving Manager has since been less prolific in his imaginative announcements.

AT the Cheltenham Police Court on Monday, Charles Henry Hodson, aged twenty-four, Theatrical performer, was charged with stealing a gold Geneva watch from the person of "Miss Lillie Lonsdale," at the Theatre Royal, on the 8th inst.; and also with wilfully breaking a pier glass, of the value of £4 10s., the property of Miss Lonsdale. Mr Chesshyre prosecuted, and Mr Marshall defended the accused.

Prosecutrix said she was the wife of Robert James Alexander Cyrim Wilson. She was Lessee of the Theatre Royal, Old Wells, and was now living at 29, Cambray. She had had a dispute with the accused about his salary, and on Saturday night, while she was in the act of lighting the gas in the green-room, the prisoner snatched her watch. As he was leaving the room, he was stopped, and the watch fell on the floor. The prisoner then smashed a large pier glass, which was lying on the floor. In reply to a question by Mr Marshall, as to whether she had not thrashed the prisoner, Miss Lonsdale said, "During the morning performance, while I was dressing for the character of Myles-na-Coppaleen, Mr Hodson came to the green-room door, and sent in a note to me, asking for payment of his wages before treasury. I sent back the note, with my answer, "No." I heard the prisoner call out, "Then I will not go on with my part." I came out of my room partially dressed, and said to Mr Hodson, "You won't perform your part?" He said, "No, I will not." I then called Mr Courtnay, the Stage Manager, and told him what had occurred, and he said he thought the prisoner ought to play his part. I again asked him if he would go on with his part. He said, "No, I will not, unless you will place my salary in the hands of Mr Courtnay." He also said something to the effect that he did not trust me with the money, or that I could not pay him. I seized him by the collar, and ordered him to leave the Theatre instantly. He asked me who I was, and what I had to do with him, and, holding a whip over my head, said, "D---- you, I'll smash you." Mr Courtnay was standing by with a stick in his hand, which I seized, and gave the prisoner a sound beating. I then went to the proscenium and apologised to the audience for the defendant's absence. I engaged another person to take his part, and gave him 10s. for doing so."

In reply to Mr Marshall, witness said she would admit thrashing the prisoner, and would do the same to a dozen such men were they to insult her as he did.

Other evidence was tendered, but at the close of the case the Bench were of the opinion there was no felonious intention, and dismissed the case.

The charge of wilfully breaking the pier glass was then gone into. The evidence was the same as in the former case, and the Bench ordered the defendant to pay £4 1s. damages, 10s. fine, with 6s. 6d. costs, in default of one month's imprisonment. The money was paid.

16/4/1865

The Assassination of Abraham Lincoln.
TO THE EDITOR OF THE ERA.
Dear Sir, – I trust that immediate steps will be taken by some of our foremost men in the dramatic art, in London and in the provinces, to procure the signature of every actor in the United Kingdom to a document expressing their horror and their indignation at the atrocious deed, committed by one whose name will be forever execrated by every member of the profession. I am, Sir, yours in great sorrow, JAMES BENNETT. Stratford-on-Avon, April 27th, 1865.

30/4/1865

COPYRIGHT – "JOLLY DOGS."
COURT OF COMMON PLEAS.
D'ALCORN v. SHEARD. – This was an action to recover damages for an alleged infringement of copyright in the popular song known as "Jolly Dogs," or "Slap Bang."

Mr Hawkins, Q.C., and Mr Charles Russell appeared for the plaintiff; Mr Henry James for the defendant.

Mr Hawkins said the plaintiff was a music publisher in Rathbone Place, and the defendant carried on a similar business in Holborn. In October, 1864, the plaintiff bought the copyright of the song in question of Mr Harry Copeland, who composed it, and at great expense the plaintiff bought brought the song fully before the public notice. The "Great Vance" was induced to sing it, and it was now a most popular song. The full name of the song was "Jolly Dogs! We Are All Jolly Dogs! Such Jolly Dogs Are We; or, Slap, Bang! Here We Are Again!" and in February, 1865, the defendant published a polka called the "Slap, Bang, Here We Are Again Polka," and in the course of the dance the dancers were to sing "Slap, Bang, Here We Are Again! What Jolly Dogs Are We!" The plaintiff did not claim any copyright in the music, but the infringement that he complained of was the use of the words similar to those of his song.

Mr D'Alcorn, the plaintiff, said that he had spent upwards of £100 in bringing out his song before the public. The selling price was 1s. 3d. a copy, the cost being about three halfpence. The defendant published his polka at 6d. The sale of the song rose from 200 a week in October to 600 in February, and afterwards rapidly sank until it got down to 100 in May. He had himself sold permission to a person to publish a "Slap, Bang Polka" for ten guineas, and had refused the offer of £21 for permission to publish a set of quadrilles with the same title. He thought his copyright was worth £300, and that it would have been worth £300 to £400 had it not been injured by the defendant's publication.

Mr Harry Copeland* said that he composed the song. It had attained great popularity, a fact which did not say much for the taste of the British public, for though he had written 100 songs this was the worst of them all. (Laughter.)

Mr Hawkins – If the subject had sung your best, then it must have driven them mad with ecstasy. (Renewed laughter.) What is your best?

Witness – I think the one founded upon Mr Sala's story of "Twice Round the Clock."

Mr Hawkins – What do you call it? Witness – I call it "London."

Mr Hawkins (to his junior) – Make a note of that. (Loud laughter.)

Cross-examined – He frequently heard the air played in the streets, much to his annoyance.

Mr James – Annoyance! Why, I should have thought it immortality.

Witness continued – He first sang it in Dublin in January, 1864, but the medical students kicked up such a row, and broke so many glasses, that he was not allowed to continue singing it. (Laughter.) He afterwards sang it at Brighton, where it was a hit. He sold the copyright of it to the plaintiff for a guinea, and thought himself remarkably well paid (laughter), but he should add that the plaintiff had given him several pounds since in consequence of the great popularity and sale of the song.

Mr Pennikett and Mr Vance, comic singers; Mr W. West, a delineator of Negro character and stump orator; Mr Bernard Isaacson, musical director; and Mr W.B. Wright, comedian, were examined upon the question of copyright in the song, and also in reference to its popularity, and the damage done by the defendant in publication.

In cross-examination it was stated that the music was almost identical with that of an obscure song called "The Bungalow," Questions were also asked with the view of showing that words similar to the refrain of the plaintiff's song had sometimes been used when singing "The Bungalow" in a song called "Slap, Bang, or the Adventures of Solomon Slip Stitch," and in the Pantomime of *Hey Diddle Diddle*, performed at the Surrey Theatre. Most of the witnesses denied knowledge of the circumstances suggested by the questions, or distinguished the plaintiff's song from the other compositions.

At the conclusion of the plaintiff's case the further hearing was adjourned until this (Saturday) morning.

To Lessees, Managers, &c. WANTED, by a Young Farmer, who has never seen a Greenroom or been on any Stage, EMPLOY in connection with one of the leading Theatres, where he could introduce Original and adapted Classic Drama, subject only to a participation on success. See his first and unrevised Play, PARTHENIA PICKERING, printed (printer's errors excepted) as written when a Ploughboy. Address, Author, 18, Rich Terrace, Brompton.
28/5/1865

TO THE EDITOR OF THE ERA.
A Wonderful Living Skeleton.
MR EDITOR. – At Glasgow Fair there has been exhibiting a "living being" under the above cognomen. Curiosity led us into the exhibition, but, when once within the precincts of the show, would have given thrice the sum paid for admission to have been out again, for there indeed was a human being, who grinned his smiles to us in a manner not by any means pleasant to view, in fact a head without flesh, its bones seemingly held together by merely a tight fitting skin. Its skeleton body was also exhibited, and was in perfect accordance with its barebone head, and wore the same appearance as the skeleton in any anatomical exhibition; and yet it talked, walked, laughed, and lived, and strange to say, was jocular, healthy, and intelligent. The name of this monstrosity is Robert Tipney, a native of March, in Cambridgeshire, and is exhibited by the proprietor, a Mr Chipperfield. It is astonishing to see the crowds who rushed to see this living anatomy. I acknowledge the sight, though extraordinary, was by no means pleasing to my view, but those who take pleasure in seeing such unusual monstrosities would do well to guard against imposition, as the great success of Chipperfield's exhibition has induced not over-scrupulous showmen to secure poor, consumptive, half-starved wretches, whom they exhibit for the reality. Your obedient servant, D.P.M.
23/7/1865

IF the ENTHUSIASTIC INDIVIDUAL who distinguished himself on the PLATFORM of ANERLEY GARDENS on Wednesday last can be warranted sober and guaranteed an umbrella, in the use of which he is decidedly unrivalled, he is requested to apply to the Treasurer any Monday evening, when he will hear of something to his "advantage."
30/7/1865

THE BABY ACTRESS. – In conjunction with her father, Mr Alfred Howard, who gave some dramatic recitals and comic sketches, this juvenile wonder appeared at the Marylebone Institution on Wednesday evening last. We have already spoken of the extraordinary talent possessed by the above child (not yet two years of age), and our remarks were fully bourne out by her performance in the presence of the London public. Her tender age being taken into consideration, her actual articulation is remarkably perfect, and the speeches she utters are beyond question, accompanied with appropriate action. This is something very remarkable, and almost surpasses belief until personal experience removes every particle of doubt. She took part in a scene from *King John*, and gave the text in an extraordinarily perfect manner. Little Miss Howard's accomplishments are various, for in addition to her dramatic venture she gave specimens of her capability as a dancer and singer, as well as a short account of her late visit to Glasgow. The means whereby this surprising result has been achieved are, of course, known only to Mr Howard, her father and preceptor.
6/8/1865

A FEARFUL scene occurred at the Lyceum Theatre, Sunderland, on Thursday night, during the performance of the Pantomime *Robin Hood*. A gutta-percha tube connecting the wing lights became detached, and the gas escaping, ignited, and a loud explosion took place, the flames shooting up to the top of the stage. A rush was made to the door by the audience, who thought the Theatre was on fire, but they were stopped by seeing Miss Louisa Ricardo*, who was engaged as Columbine Watteau, rush on to the stage enveloped in flames. She had been standing amongst a group collected at the wing, waiting her turn to go on, when the flames caught her muslin skirt. She shrieked and rushed on in the middle of the scene, where her father was playing as Clown, but was thrown down by one of the stage carpenters. Mr Bell, the Lessee, rushed from his private box, and his top coat was pulled off and wrapped round the poor girl and the flames were beaten out. A number of the audience clambered from the pit to the stage while the fearful scene was going on, but they ultimately resumed their seats, and the performance proceeded.

Miss Ricardo was removed home and attended to by medical men, and on Friday morning no dangerous results were apprehended, though she was sadly burnt about the arms and chest. She died, however, at two o'clock in the afternoon from her injuries and the shock to her system. Her father was so much burned in endeavouring to put out the fire that he will be unable to resume his profession for some time.

*Louisa was only twelve years old.
31/12/1865

7
1866
UNIQUE FISH DRESSES

FIRE! FIRE! FIRE! – TO MANAGERS – If you want to preserve your expensive Scenery and Properties untarnished, use WINDER'S COLOURED FIRES; if you don't want to suffocate the Workmen in the Flies use Winder's Coloured Fires; if you wish your Pantomimists to breathe freely after their first rally, use Winder's Coloured Fires; if you don't wish to set the asthmatical portion of the Audience coughing, use Winder's Coloured Fires; if you wish a brilliant and powerful Light upon everything, use Winder's Coloured Fires; if you wish to save 20 per cent. in the price, use Winder's Coloured Fires; and if you don't wish to upset or waste the above, use TANNER'S IMPROVED FIRE BOXES, with Lid Fastening and Moveable Reflector. Sole agents in London, TANNER and PARKES, 66, Hercules Buildings, Lambeth. N.B., in a few days the Prismatic Torrent, patented.
18/2/1866

MR EDITOR. – Sir, – As you stand up for the rights of Professionals, I trust you will grant me a small space in your paper to plead the rights of audiences. A couple of Highland dancers appeared for the *first time* on Monday night at the Cambridge Music Hall here. They danced, were encored, and danced again, and, in answer to the *slightest call*, appeared for the third time and thanked the audience for the kind manner in which they had received them, and *begged to inform them that Friday next was set apart for their benefit, and trusted their friends would rally round them and give them a bumper*, and they have gone through the same humiliating farce each night so far. Now, Sir, I don't propose to teach such Professionals self-respect, but I do urge that audiences have a right to hiss down such inflictions as these. The publication of this note may abate the evil. ONE OF THE GODS, Huddersfield, Feb. 23rd, 1866.
25/2/1866

FOR SALE, a LIVING CURIOSITY, a CLEVER SHEEP, with Five Legs; Dances, fires off a Pistol, &c., &c. Apply to J.G.L., 10, Cold Harbour, Margate.
8/4/1866

Ira Aldridge at Constantinople.
THE celebrated African tragedian has recently been starring it in the Ottoman capital, where, for the first time in the City of the Sultan, the works of the immortal Shakespeare were presented, the leading characters by Ira Aldridge in their original tongue, while the other parts were given in French. The performances took place in the handsome French Theatre of Pera, and notwithstanding the great difficulty of having two languages used (English and French) the experiment was no less novel than successful, the house being densely crowded every night Mr Aldridge appeared. The members of the

Corps Diplomatique, the Ministers, Chamberlains, and other members of the Sultan's household, as well as the elite of the capital, enjoyed the masterly delineations of Ira Aldridge with as keen a zest, if not as full an appreciation, as the most critical English audience. It will be interesting to know what a remarkable success attended these representations, and it is needless to say that the most convincing proof of the genius of the tragedian in his portrayal of Othello, Shylock, Macbeth, and his other parts, lies in the circumstances that, although a large portion of those present did not understand the language used, they thoroughly realised the grandeur, force, and expression with which the talented actor sustained the characters. [...]

In consequence of previously-arranged engagements in Russia – where Mr Aldridge enjoys a very great popularity – he was unable to protract his stay in Constantinople longer than a fortnight. The Sultan was out of town, and notwithstanding the pressing request to remain, it was impossible for Mr Aldridge, on this occasion, to stop in order to perform before his Majesty in his magnificent private Theatre – perhaps the most superb building of the kind in existence, it having been erected by the late Sultan at a cost of some hundred thousands of pounds. It is understood that, at the completion of his Russian tour, Mr Aldridge will again make his appearance before a Turkish audience, with whom his fame is now well established. According to the last accounts received, he was at Kertch, where he was playing to full houses. After visiting the Crimea, and performing in the large towns of Southern Russia, he will appear at Moscow and St. Petersburgh, where his popularity is also well established. The Emperor of Russia has decorated this celebrated actor with the orders of Stanislaus and St. Anne. Mr Aldridge had previously received decorations from the chief sovereigns of Europe.
6/5/1866

INCLINATION TO SLEEP AFTER DINNER shows a weak digestion, and it should be prevented, as it may be readily, by taking two or three of PARR'S LIFE PILLS at night, or one before dinner occasionally. May be had of any Chemist.
10/6/1866

Atrocious Case of Cruelty to an Artist.
THE world is truly said to contain many murderers whose crimes remain for years unpunished. Retribution follows, sometimes slowly and surely, and sometimes with a sudden swoop, all those incarnations of malice and treachery, who stop short of actual blood shedding, but attack a man in the most miserable and cowardly manner through those bound to him by the strongest domestic ties. We briefly lay before our readers the circumstances of a fiendish piece of cruelty we trust, for the credit of common humanity, [to be] without parallel.

William Talliott, gymnast and acrobat (one of the well-known Talliott Brothers), dislocated his neck while fulfilling an engagement at Copenhagen last year. The brain has since become gradually affected, and while fulfilling an engagement with Mr C. Hengler at Birmingham poor Talliott's malady increased. Mrs Talliott being engaged in Mr John Henderson's troupe at Brighton, sent for her husband, and consulted several medical men as to the prospect of his recovery. She was told his case was hopeless, and this fact would have secured to her the pity of all but brutes in whom the ordinary feelings of humanity have no place. Mrs Talliott accompanied Mr Henderson's Circus to Stratford, where she worked hard to gain a subsistence for herself, and to keep her husband at Brighton for the benefit of sea air. This separation seems to have given some fiend in human shape an idea which the vilest at Portland or Toulon would shrink from carrying into effect. William Talliott received a Post-office order in his wife's name, and also a letter stating that her legs were broken through a horse having fallen upon her. The husband came immediately to Stratford, and finding her safe took his farewell of her in this world, for the excitement and shock to his feelings drove him mad. He is now in a Lunatic Asylum, and he or she who is the chief cause of this awful affliction is unfortunately at large.

The circumstances are too solemn and too serious for the whole affair to bear the usual "practical joking" interpretation. As showing the lengths to which deliberate, remorseless, and pitiless malice will go, this incident is almost incredible. If a man, the author of this misery may well be called a "kindless villain." That any woman could so have belied her name and disgraced her sex surpasses belief. Having stated the facts to our Professional readers we make no appeal for material assistance on behalf of poor William Tallott. We can anticipate the sentiments of horror and indignation which will be felt upon the perusal of this mournful story, and we beg merely to make one suggestion to every follower of Talliott's craft. It is that they should use their utmost endeavours to discover and impeach the individual who has committed this foul outrage. Let the man or woman on whose soul lies this shameful crime be hunted down, and their names execrated by the entire Profession, for some justice should be done to William Talliott, who now suffers from the heartlessness of some wretch "whom it were charity to call a coward."
8/7/1866

THE NEGRO BOY PIANIST. – Blind Tom, the musical prodigy, who has created so great a sensation throughout the United States, has arrived in England and will, we understand, shortly make his appearance in public. His execution of the most difficult music is a perfect marvel. Blind and untaught he plays the most brilliant pieces, and the extraordinary retention in his memory of any composition he may have heard, and which he at once repeats with faultless precision, has gained for him the title of a musical monstrosity.
15/7/1866

TO THE EDITOR OF THE ERA.
Sir, – In your last issue I notice a letter from Mr H.G. Mapleson, complaining of a criticism of mine which appeared in *The Era* of the 5th inst., in which I observed that "On Wednesday *Othello* was performed for the first time this season, in order to give an *amateur* (Mr H.G. Mapleson) an opportunity of making himself ridiculous as the Moor." Mr Mapleson complains that I called him an "amateur;" he goes on to state that he has played Othello about two hundred times "without a dissentient voice," and he says that he "does not consider himself an amateur." I neither know nor care what Mr Mapleson "considers" himself; but this I know, that he was *announced* as an *amateur* in the advertisements of the performance. I have before me the *Isle of Man Times* containing an advertisement of the performances at the Theatre Royal, in which appear the following words: – "On Wednesday, *Othello*. Othello (on this occasion) by a *distinguished amateur*." Am I to blame for calling him an "amateur", when he allows himself to be denominated such in the announcements of his performance?

As to what Mr Mapleson "considers" himself, with that I have nothing to do. Some persons are given to thinking very highly of themselves, and Mr Mapleson may "consider" himself a very clever tragedian, and altogether a star of the greatest magnitude, because, as he states, he has played with T.C. King, J. Wallack, John Vandenhoff, and "many other men of ability;" but because he is vain enough to rate his talents highly, that is no proof whatever that he worthily fills the high pinnacle on which he apparently seeks to perch himself. He says that when he played Othello on this occasion "the house was crammed from the floor to the ceiling with a most attentive audience, and I was most enthusiastically received during the entire play, and called before the curtain at its conclusion." Admitting all this, I venture to assert that the house was not "crammed" because this "distinguished amateur" was announced to play the Moor, but because this being the height of the season the house is nightly filled, no matter how miserable the entertainments announced may be. No doubt great enthusiasm was manifested "during the entire play," but it appears to me that the lion's share of that enthusiasm was due, not to the "distinguished amateur," but to the admirable acting of Mr Fernandez (a very clever gentleman) as Iago. Certainly, Mr Mapleson *appeared* "before the curtain" at the conclusion of the piece, but I question very much that he was *called* "before the curtain." On the contrary, that "call" appeared to me to have been

intended for Mr Fernandez, and not for the "distinguished amateur," who showed on that occasion that he did not hesitate to appropriate to himself an honour that was intended for a gentleman that possessed infinitely more ability, and far more modesty, than he does. With regard to Mr Mapleson's having been "informed that I was not in the house on the occasion" of his appearance as Othello, all I can say is, simply that his information is not correct. – Yours truly, YOUR CORRESPONDENT IN THE ISLE OF MAN. August 15th, 1866.
19/8/1866

TO MANAGERS. – CHRISTMAS PANTOMIME. – FOR SALE, the Splendid and Unique FISH DRESSES, made in Paris, the Marvellous Set of CHESS MEN, the Beautiful TRANSFORMATION, and BALLET DRESSES, &c. The Highly Successful Pantomime of KING CHESS; or, Tom the Piper's Son, can be played on moderate terms. Apply to Messrs SHEPHERD and CRESWICK, New Surrey Theatre, London.
30/9/1866

MELANCHOLY END OF A MUSICAL ENGAGEMENT. – A deplorable accident occurred at Stonebridge, near Hampton-in-Arden, on Wednesday morning. On Tuesday morning the band of the 1st Warwickshire Militia, consisting of thirteen performers, proceeded to Maxstoke Castle, near Coleshill, having been engaged to take part in the festivities given in honour of the marriage of Fetherstone Dilke*, Esq., who had returned that day from his wedding tour. At about half-past ten o'clock on the following morning the return journey was commenced, and a number of the men were seated outside of the vehicle, amongst whom was the unfortunate deceased, William Blakeman. While descending a hill near Stonebridge the horses suddenly took fright, and deceased was thrown head foremost into the turnpike-road. Many of the other men were also thrown from the vehicle, and received severe contusions. Blakeman was immediately picked up and conveyed to a public-house. The body was found to be perfectly inanimate, the deceased having sustained a contusion of the brain. The unfortunate man, who was forty years of age, has left a wife and five children behind him.
Editor's note: Mr Dilke's marriage to Rosamond, daughter of Sir Alexander and Lady Maria Dixie, was not a happy one. In 1877 Mr Dilke killed himself by cutting his throat in an Ilfracombe hotel, and in 1881 Rosamond gave birth to Harold Heneage Dilke, who was probably the son of her old flame Joseph Heneage Finch, 7th Earl of Aylesford. In 1915 Harold married my great-great aunt Amelia Edwards.
21/10/1866

NEW GAS LIGHTING FOR THEATRES. – The new Prince of Wales Theatre, at Liverpool, is admirably lighted, and deserves a word of praise. The footlights are on an entirely new principle, by which the audience will not be able to see any glare or flicker, and the heated air will be carried away by a flue provided for the purpose. Over the lights is placed a fire-proof composition, so that the ballet girls run no danger of fire; while the lights are on a level with the stage, thus throwing no obstacle in the way of a perfect view from any part of the house. By an ingenious plan, too, red, green, and other shades of colour can be thrown upon the stage by a sort of cylindrical movement of coloured glass over the footlights, so that the good old system of red or green fire in the transformation and other scenes will be entirely done away with. This is a plan suggested and patented by Messrs Defries and Co., of Houndsditch, London.
28/10/1866

TO THE EDITOR OF THE ERA.
Sir, – I know not to whom else I can address my complaint.
This evening (Wednesday) three swells in their own conceit, but arrant snobs, I warrant you, interrupted everyone leaving the Prince of Wales's Theatre at the close of the performance whilst they in turn lighted their cigars at one of the gas lights in the dress circle passage, and continued smoking, to the great annoyance of several ladies, until they reached the entrance door.

I looked for some of the box-keepers and attendants, but could not see any of them. For thirty years I have been a frequent visitor to the Theatres, but this is the first time I have seen a cigar lighted within the walls of a Theatre.

It may, perhaps, be the "correct thing" to light cigars inside a Music Hall, and possibly these three snobs (for gentlemen I cannot call them) forgot they were in a Theatre; but there are some people so selfish that they care not what annoyance they inflict on others, and these cigar-lighters may form part of that family.

If you will kindly publish this letter I have no doubt it will prevent a repetition of this nuisance. Your obedient servant, R. Oct. 31st.
4/11/1866

BEAUTIFUL LIZZIE, in GLASGOW, Delighting Fashionable and Crowded Audiences at the WHITEBAIT ROOMS. The Newcastle Paper, September 15th, 1866, says: – They ca her bonnie Lizzie. Sor she's tornd twenty-one, she's mayd like a Fairy, she has leet flaxy hair, blue peepers, an a pair o cheeks like rosis; she nocks Tom Thumb an Minny Worrin into convulshins, sor.
18/11/1866

AT West Hartlepool, on Saturday night, some excitement was caused in consequence of a report that Mr Charles Verner, the Lessee of the Theatre Royal, West Hartlepool, had committed suicide. It appears that, about five o'clock, Mr Verner had purchased two ounces of laudanum, stating that he wanted to saturate lint. But Mr Verner left the shop, returned to his residence, and almost immediately swallowed the whole contents of the bottle. After he had done so he told his wife, who immediately ran for medical assistance. Dr Gourley attended with a stomach pump, but Mr Verner was not willing that it should be used. On the tube being inserted in his mouth, he tore and bit it, and resisted as much as he could. Dr Gourley left him and went for assistance. Sergeant Kirby and another officer were summoned, and a metal tube stomach pump was borrowed from another medical man, and, by the assistance of the police, the contents of Mr Verner's stomach were emptied, and he recovered in a short time. He then said that he had taken the laudanum in mistake for brandy. – From the *Leeds Mercury*, Tuesday, the 20th inst.
25/11/1866

RESCUE OF A BOY BY A THEATRICAL DOG. – Last Wednesday afternoon, while a boy was fishing near the docks at Dundee, he suddenly hauled up his line, thinking there was a fish on it. In the hurry and excitement, the little fellow lost his balance, and fell into the water. At the time, Mr Harrison, of the Dundee Music Hall, happened to be passing with one of his large sagacious dogs. He instantly directed the attention of the animal to the condition of the boy. It jumped into the water at once, and brought the boy safely to shore in a very few seconds after the accident occurred.
2/12/1866

The Misfortunes of Three Ballet Girls in New York.
TO THE EDITOR OF THE NEW YORK HERALD.
Knowing the interest you take in all that concerns the Drama and its professors, no matter how humble, we venture to address you on a matter that affects us nearly. At present we are but humble members of the Theatre, but even we have rights, which we believe to have been deliberately invaded. We are three English girls, members of the *corps de ballet* at Wheatley's Theatre, and are at present appearing nightly in the ballet.

In the early part of the present year Messres J----- and P-----, who were then in England, invited us to proceed to New York, and offered us respectively salaries of £3 per week. On making out our agreements, knowing our utter ignorance of the true value of American money, instead of inserting "three pounds sterling," as they distinctly promised us, they inserted the amount, fifteen dollars, which is the sum we are now receiving weekly, and which, in spite of repeated and earnest solicitations, they insist on paying us.

On our arrival in New York we found that it takes seven dollars in greenbacks to make an English sovereign, and although we are in justice and honour bound to receive twenty-one dollars (having solemnly been promised the value of £3) we continue to receive but fifteen dollars. It is a well known fact that Messrs J----- and P----- are clearing a large sum weekly by their share in the Theatre, and it seems a hard case that we three girls, with no other resources to depend on save and except the salary produced by our dancing, should each have to lose weekly six dollars, and we think it most unworthy on the part of J----- and P----- to delude young girls from their homes in England by false representations as to the relative value of money. The fifteen dollars we are now receiving amount to about £2 4s., a very little more than our salary was in England, and it is not likely that we would cross the ocean and make a journey of over three thousand miles to better ourselves a few shillings per week. When J----- and P----- engaged us they knew perfectly well that five dollars did not represent a sovereign, but they repeatedly assured us that the two amounts were equal.

At the present rate of living in New York, what with high rents and the dearness of provisions, this difference of six dollars a week would purchase us many little comforts. As to saving anything out of our present salary, that is entirely out of the question. In making their engagements J----- and P----- were careful not to inform us that the cost of living was dearer in New York than in England. Here again they benefitted by our inexperience.

We are very sorry, Mr Editor, to have to be compelled to appeal to the public Press to make our voices heard; but will you argue our claim with the Crook-ed speculators of the *corps de ballet*? Winter is fast approaching. The extra money to which we are entitled would purchase us some warm clothing, of which we are sorely in need. As we said before, we depend wholly and solely upon our salaries; and if you can spare us the humiliation of of having to pledge our little finery and bits of jewellery that we brought with us from England, we shall indeed feel grateful.

Messrs J----- and P-----, secure in their prosperity, may reply that they are fulfilling their contract by paying us fifteen dollars a week. Our reply is that we were told by these men that fifteen dollars was the same as £3. We now know that our just salary is twenty-one dollars currency, and with nothing short of this will we be content.
ELISE BURLINGHAM
ANNIE P. COOKE
ROSE RYAN

Theatre Royal New Concert Hall, St Helens, Lancashire.
WANTED, an Instructor for a Duffer, who is assuming the Name of a Clever Person. Good Talent Wanted. Will MISS LIZZIE HARRIS please write in. Address, JAMES FIDLER.
9/12/1866

The Death in the Circus at the Agricultural Hall.
Yesterday (Saturday) afternoon Dr Edward Lankester, the Coroner for Central Middlesex, presided over a Jury at the King's Head Tavern, Upper-street, Islington, to inquire into the circumstances relative to the death of Samuel Gibson, a groom in the employ of Mr G. Sanger, Propreitor of "Sanger's Circus and Menagerie," now exhibiting at the Agricultural Hall.

The Jury having viewed the body, Mr G. Sanger, in the absence of the father of the deceased, gave evidence of identification, and proceeded by saying that he was known all over the world, but his place of nativity was Newbery, in Berkshire; but he at the present time was Proprietor of the Circus, at the Agricultural Hall. The deceased had been in his employ about ten months as groom, and took charge of four or five horses. He had a salary of 18s. a week, and besides attending to the horses he had to make himself generally useful in the Circus. Witness did not see the accident. He was called just afterwards, and saw deceased in the stable. He felt his pulse, and was of the opinion that he was dead. He did not think that blame was attached to any party.

By the Coroner – Since deceased had been in witness's employ, he had never been the worse for drink.

By a Juror – The deceased was leading one of the nine horses attached to a triumphal car which was performing in the circle. The horses were three abreast, and were going at the rate of three miles an hour. Deceased had charge of one of the horses. There were six grooms to the nine horses, and the length of the carriage was from eighteen to twenty feet. The accident did not occur at the turning of the arena, but opposite the stables. The same carriage had been driven at a much more rapid rate. Witness had been sixteen years an equestrian manager, and in his companies a fatal accident had never before occurred.

Alfred Coningham, in the service of Mr Sanger, said that about half-past nine on Wednesday evening last he was engaged as one of the grooms attending nine horses attached to a triumphal car. He was on the off side, and behind deceased, but on the same side of the carriage. They had been round the circle twice, and, while going the third time, the deceased fell and appeared to roll among the horses, and under their feet. If witness had fallen he would have rolled away. The fore and hind wheels passed over his body.

By the Coroner – The rate at which they were going was four of five miles an hour. Witness did not think anyone was to blame. When deceased fell witness was confused, but he thought that some of the audience got into the circle to assist deceased.

To a Juror – Witness had seen such carriages go at a much quicker rate, and in a much smaller space.

Mr Sanger – Oh, yes. Nine or ten miles an hour.

By a Juror – Witness did not assist the deceased. He left him lying where he fell. No-one but the audience assisted. Witness went to fetch Mr Sanger. He was excited. He was the elephant keeper. He did all he could to assist the deceased, to the best of his ability. Deceased seemed bewildered.

By another Juror – The two wheels on one side of the carriage passed over deceased. It was going a straight road, near the orchestra, and was not on a turn.

Mr C. Greene, who was present, witnessing the performance, said he was on the opposite side of the Hall, but saw the man fall, but from what circumstance he could not say. He was surprised to hear the pace to be said that of three or four miles. It seemed to him to be impossible. It was about two or three miles an hour.

By a Juror – It certainly was not a dangerous pace, and the car had passed round the curve and was in the straight line. He could not say what was the cause of the accident. He had seen the performance once or twice before. The audience by their feeling of loyalty were led to ask the procession to go round a third time. There was a great feeling of excitement.

By a Juror – Witness was not a shareholder. He attended professionally.

Mr William Butler, surgeon, deposed that his assistant attended deceased, and found him dead. He (witness) had made a *post-mortem* examination, and found externally some slight abrasions on the neck and face. The right thigh was fractured, and there was a bruise on the groin. Internally there was congestion of the brain. The second and third ribs on the left side were broken, but did not cause any laceration of the lungs or other viscera. There was blood in the pelvis, but no fracture of the pelvis. He believed it was a case of sudden death, and that deceased had not been run over, but kicked by the horses.

By the Coroner – Witness believed the congestion of the brain produced death. The heart was healthy. Deceased might have fallen from giddiness. The injuries to the chest might have accelerated death. The going round the third time might have accelerated death from the excitement after previous exhaustion.

The Coroner made some remarks as to the public wishing to see and enjoying hair-breadth escapes and dangerous performances, and, having once seen it, required an encore, producing excitement on the part of the performers.

A Juror asked Mr Sanger the weight of the triumphal car, and being answered "Five tons," they were generally of the opinion that the rate at which they were going round the circle was far too great.

The Coroner then summed up, and left the Jury to consider their verdict.

After a short consultation, a verdict of "Accidental Death" was returned, with an expression of opinion that such processions should not move so fast, and that on no occasion should there be a repetition of exhibitions wherein exhaustion and excitement were created were created in the performance.

The Inquiry then closed.

PIETRO CARLE, the Great Clown, who has won for himself such wondrous renown. This year LIVERPOOL is his location, where, in the minds of the public, he has caused a sensation. He can Dance, Sing, and Act, likewise play on a Trumpet, and, in his Hornpipe on Pattens, doesn't he stump it? His dresses are new, and best patterns made, which entirely throws all the rest in the shade; but he does not believe in that work they call spangling, 'cause when they're sent to the wash they get spoilt in the mangling; but with that famed Pantaloon, W. Butler, by his side, in Pantomimical Freaks, competition's defied. – (Signed) – PIETRO CARLE, Clown, Royal Colosseum Theatre, Liverpool.
30/12/1866

8
1867
ACROBATIC FATHERS, BE KIND TO YOUR KIDS

PRESENTATION TO A DONKEY. – On Monday last Mr W.H. Payne, the pantomimist, presented to the Fore and Hind Legs of his Donkey two handsome Silver Medals, for their strict attention to his training and instruction. The medals were manufactured by Messrs Loewenstark and Sons, Masonic Jewellers, of Garrick-street, and bore the following inscription: – "Presented by W.H. Payne, of the Theatre Royal, Covent-garden, to Master William Allcroft and Master John Mapstone in remembrance of his donkey, Ali Baba, 1866 and 1867." They were received by the Legs with kicks of delight and rapture.
20/1/1867

SCANDALOUS CONDUCT AT THE LICENSED VICTUALLERS' BALL. – On Thursday night, during the time that the Licensed Victuallers' Ball was taking place at St James's Hall, some miscreant threw on the floor some stuff – supposed to be a mixture of pepper with some other ingredient – which had the effect of setting the persons assembled sneezing and coughing, so much so that some of them were unable to remain in the room. It having been represented to the officials what had occurred, a reward of £20 was offered to anyone who could discover the offender, but, unfortunately, without success.

EXTRAORDINARY DIVORCE CASE. – HANCOCK v. PEATY.
The Queen's Advocate (Sir R. Phillmore) and Dr Tristram appeared, at the Court of Divorce, for the petitioner, and Dr Spinks, Q.C., and Mr Searle appeared for the defendant.

This was a very extraordinary case, being a petition for dissolution of marriage, presented to the Court by the guardian of a young lady, on the ground that she was insane at the time the marriage took place to the respondent. The case occupied the Court the whole of Friday, and was resumed yesterday. The facts are these: – Miss Mary Ann Hancock was the youngest daughter of a manufacturer, residing in London, who died in 1835, leaving a widow and several children. The widow lived until 1852, when she died from insanity. The respondent in this case, Mr Peaty, is a clerk in the Bank of England, and is cousin to Miss Hancock, and for some time he paid his addresses to her. Long before the marriage, Miss Hancock had been the subject of curious delusions, at various intervals, and she was looked upon in the family as a person of unsound mind. She dressed herself in peculiar ways, and wore her hair in a most disorderly fashion. In spite of the remonstrances of the family, and also some medical men, Mr Peaty persisted in marrying Miss Hancock. When told that she was mad, he said, if that was really the case, she was only mad through love for him.

Two or three days prior to the marriage taking place she sat for a long time in a bath in a state of nudity, looking at the drawing of a bridge which she had pinned upon the wall, and under which she said her and her intended husband must pass before they could be married. It was only by the greatest persuasion she was got out of this bath and some articles of clothing put round her. She laboured under many delusions, such as, for instance, that she was a person of the greatest importance in the political world, and had some great mission to perform. She thought her food was poisoned, and many times refused to partake of it. In spite of all these things, however, Mr Peaty demanded that a marriage should take place, and accordingly, in August 1863, the two were married at St Mathias's Church, Paddington. During the ceremony Miss Hancock conducted herself in a most extraordinary manner, and when in the vestry of the church she wished to enter into an argument with the clergyman as to the relations between Church and State. After a short wedding tour, in which Scarborough was visited, Mr and Mrs Peaty returned to London, and took up their residence in Osnaburgh-terrace, but only three weeks had elapsed when she had to be placed under restraint, and she was ultimately removed to St Luke's Asylum, where she remained for a considerable period. Since the marriage she had become entitled to about £3,000.

Amongst the witnesses who were called on Friday were Dr Cumming of Chelsea, the medical attendant of the lady, who said she was undoubtedly mad, and not fit to marry. Miss Harriet Hancock, sister to Mrs Peaty, described at great length the peculiarities under which her sister laboured. She would sit in her bedroom all day, and sometimes decline to take her meals. She said that the society was not good enough for her, though it consisted of her own sisters. She said that some one had offended her out of doors, and she found it necessary to punish the whole family severely. Her behaviour at meals was very strange; she seemed to be trembling with passion, and to strike her plate violently with her knife. Her dress was peculiar. She piled her hair high upon her head, and put ribbons on top of this hair, and then over all there was a bonnet quite a quarter of a yard high in the air. When remonstrated with for this she remarked that all her tendencies were "upwards," and she persisted in keeping to the style. She refused to wash herself, stating that she was too pure to need washing. She would go for a fortnight with her face most imperfectly cleansed. She saved the water which she used stating that every part of her was too precious to be lost. At the wedding breakfast she spoke very loudly, and got up and kissed a young gentleman who was present, saying he was "a jolly good fellow." On another occasion she ran away to Brighton in her wedding dress, and was afterwards found in lodgings in that town, with the lid of a tin saucepan tied round her neck.

Dr Taylor warned Mr Peaty to be careful in marrying such a lady, but he replied that it would be all right after marriage.

Dr Ellis, of St Luke's Asylum, said Mrs Peaty was an inmate of that establishment for some time. She was taken in at the request of her husband. She laboured under numerous delusions. She said she was Princess Charlotte, and had written to the Queen. When she left St Luke's she was better than when she was admitted. Her mania must have had some hereditary taint, but it was aggravated by a disorder from which she suffered.

Mr Charles Topham, who was acquainted with Mrs Peaty before her marriage, said he was at the church when the ceremony took place. She walked into the church alone, and was in a wild and excited condition. She did not seem to be at all aware of the solemnity of the ceremony which she was going to take part in.

Dr Wood, of St Luke's Hospital, said Mrs Peaty had all the appearance of a confirmed lunatic. This was, of course, three years after the marriage.

Mrs Emma Bailey, housekeeper in the service of Dr Taylor, said she was previously with the Hancocks, and therefore knew Mrs Peaty. She was always very strange in her manner. She would get up in the middle of the night, and come downstairs in a state of nudity, and ring the bells of the house. […] The night before her marriage she said she would not marry Mr Peaty unless he would promise to read the Communion Service to her every night of her married life. She offered to marry one of Dr Taylor's pupils. A month after the marriage she went into the street in her wedding dress, and underneath this was her nightdress, and under her arm she carried a cash-box. She was ultimately prevailed upon to get into a cab. She said she had come out for a "spree," and had plenty of money. She washed a pair of gloves which had just come from the shop, saying that nothing was pure but what passed through her hands.

Mr Samuel Tryan, formerly a pupil with Dr Taylor, said he knew Mrs Peaty, and she was very eccentric in manner. On the morning of the wedding she said she thought the whole thing was a "trap," and that they were going to poison her with the breakfast. She wanted witness to either elope or marry her, but he respectfully declined. The night before her marriage she was worse than he had ever seen her before. She said all the world ought to know of her marriage, and Mr Peaty had to promise to have the bells rung. Dr Taylor strongly advised Mr Peaty, on this occasion, not to marry her, but Mr Peaty replied that if she was mad it was through extreme love for him. At the wedding breakfast she went and kissed a young gentleman who was present, and said it was entirely his own fault that he was not the bridegroom instead of Mr Peaty.

Mrs Eliza Broom, in whose house Mr and Mrs Peaty had apartments, said that on one occasion Mrs Peaty locked her husband up in the drawing-room all night. She went out at five o'clock one morning in her night attire, and did not return until eleven o'clock.

This was the case for the petitioner.

Dr Spinks, Q.C., in addressing the Court on behalf of the respondent, said this was certainly one of the most peculiar cases which had ever been before a court of law. There were no pecuniary considerations involved, for at the time this marriage took place the lady had no money, and the respondent had only £200 a year as a clerk in the Bank of England. The fact was, Mr Peaty married Miss Hancock from pure love and affection, and he believed at the time she was not insane. The lady's friends now wished that marriage to be dissolved, but as Mr Peaty had sworn at the altar to protect his wife through life he opposed this petition, hoping the Court would not take his wife away from him. Dr Spinks submitted that if his Lordship was satisfied that the lady gave her consent to this marriage it was not in the power of the Court to dissolve that contract. No doubt Mrs Peaty was eccentric in manner, but he should be able to prove by evidence that she knew perfectly well what she was doing in accepting Mr Peaty. The sisters got possession of Mrs Peaty, and, unknown to the husband, Dr Baker Brown performed an operation* upon her. It was only after this occurrence that the husband thought it best that his wife should go an asylum, where she would be properly cared for.

At the conclusion of the learned counsel's speech, the Judge suggested that the parties in this case might come to some arrangement. There appeared to be no pecuniary consideration involved, and the only object of the parties should be to have this lady properly cared for during the visitation of the dreadful malady under which she suffered. […]

Dr Lee said he had made an examination of Mrs Peaty in 1863. She was not suffering from any organic disease, but from hysteria. This hysteria appeared to be in consequence of her having conceived an affection for her cousin, which it was thought she could not carry out. He said that if any offer of marriage was made to the lady, let it not be refused, because he knew there were innumerable cases of hysteria which were never cured until the position of life was changed. There were cases, no doubt, in which marriage rather aggravated than tended to relieve this kind of hysteria. On the 17th of this month he again saw the lady, and was perfectly satisfied she was in a sound state of mind. He had also seen her again that morning. She said she was now living happily with her husband at Twickenham, and had no desire to be separated from him.

Cross-examined – He did not think this case was a very serious one, because he did not put it down in his diary of important cases at the time of the consultation with him in 1863.

The case was then adjourned until Wednesday next, in order to see whether the parties might not come to some arrangement respecting the matter.

The operation was clitoridectomy, which was believed to be a cure for hysteria. Later in 1867 Dr Baker Brown was expelled from the Obstetrical Society of London for performing the operation on women who were incapable of giving their consent.
27/1/1867

DETERMINED SUICIDE. – An inquest was held on Friday at 16, Middle Gardiner-street, Dublin, on the body of Mrs J. Scott, a young married lady, who killed herself on Thursday morning by falling from her bedroom window, on the third floor, into the street area. She had previously attempted to poison herself with laudanum, to avoid singing at an amateur concert. Dr Beattie deposed that she was of unsound mind. Verdict accordingly.

ROCHDALE. LONDON MUSIC HALL, DRAKE STREET. – The Sensation of '67! Incredible, but true! Facts speak for themselves! RELL MOREAL, the Fire Charmer, eats red hot iron, walks and jumps on red hot iron, rubs his arms, legs, face, and combs his hair with red hot iron, drinks boiling oil, washes his mouth with Molten Lead, a feat never attempted before, with various other incredible feats totally in contradiction to natural laws. These feats are no sleight of hand tricks, but are naked truth. The world beholds, struck with excitement and wonder, but cannot explain. The 'cute, the wise, the genius, may come and learn once more that wonders never cease, that we are still progressing to make even the Impossible Possible. He keeps his secret to himself, though thousands are offered for it. A few dates vacant from February 11th, prior to his American Tour. Address, MAURICE DE FRECE, Roscoe Chambers, Bold-street, Liverpool.
3/2/1867

RIMMEL'S VALENTINES. – Mr Rimmel's Valentines have a deservedly high reputation from their elegant designs and superiority of execution. Opulent swains who wish to honour their chosen ladies with offerings of this kind may disburse to the extent of £10, while less fortunate persons may pay homage both to the saint and the lady at much smaller cost. Novelties abound either at 98, Strand; 128, Regent-street; or 24, Cornhill; and the Musical Valentine is not the least among these recent and pleasant "innovations." The Musical Valentine plays a tune as soon as it is opened, and the "Medievals", designed by J. Cheret, are to be obtained at a very moderate price. The prevailing fashion of wearing stuffed birds is taken advantage of, and specimens are worked up into these 14th of February offerings. Mr Rimmel's collection is varied and rich, and will be found to satisfy all tastes.
10/2/1867

A FEMALE BARONET. – A girl named Jessie Leeson was charged at Leeds, on Saturday, with stealing a suit of men's clothes. The stolen property belonged to the son of her landlady. The girl, in a mad freak, had donned the male attire and taken up her quarters at an inn, under the name of Sir Harry Clifton, playing her part so well that for some time no suspicion arose as to her sex. Ultimately, however, the police ferreted out the secret and took her into custody. "Sir Harry" was remanded.

The Champion Giant Comic. D. LYONS, the only Giant Comic Singer ever known. A Challenge to the World, to Sing any Youth his own age and height – Seven Feet high, and Eighteen Years of age. Now at the ARGYLE MUSIC HALL, HUDDERSFIELD, where he is received with thunders of applause every night. At Liberty on the 11th March, 1867. Address as above. P.S. – Testimonials to be had of Mr Hellawell.
24/2/1867

The Law of Theatrical Engagements.
SHOREDITCH COUNTY COURT, MARCH 13.
THE BROTHER EUGENE v. POWELL AND OTHERS – THE JUDGE AND THE "TRAPEZE" PERFORMERS. – This was an action to recover one week's salary for performing on the trapeze, and damages for the detention of the trapeze and its fittings.
  Mr G.O. Nash appeared for the plaintiff, who is one of the Brothers Eugene; Mr Clark representing defendants, who are Circus proprietors, lately at the Standard.

The plaintiff, aged eighteen years, was a youth who had for some time past been known to the public as a trapeze performer, under the style of the Brother Eugene, although that was not his proper name. He had performed for the defendants at their Circus in different parts of the country, and one night at the Standard. He performed with another lad younger than himself, who was also called a Brother Eugene. The Brothers had 50s. a week, of which plaintiff kept 30s., and paid his younger professional Brother 20s.; but then he had taught the young one, brought him out, and used to buy him his "spangles." Plaintiff left defendant to fulfil another engagement, and they refused to pay him his last week.

Plaintiff's mother and father, who were very respectable people, were in court, and the mother said it was entirely against her wish that her son – her only son – carried on this life.

His Honour (Mr Dasent) – How long have you been a performer, Eugene? Plaintiff – Since I was ten years old.

His Honour – What was the commencement? Plaintiff – When I was very young I set up a pole in the garden and practiced upon it.

His Honour – And then you came out? Plaintiff – Yes.

His Honour – Don't you think you had better be at hard work? Plaintiff (smiling) – This is hard work, but I like it.

His Honour – It is very dangerous. You will be an old man before you are thirty, and you will, perhaps, meet with an accident, and then what will become of you? Plaintiff made no reply.

For the defence it was urged that the plaintiff had not served the full term of his agreement, and that the other brother was a partner in the trapeze and fittings.

The younger performer, who was still with the defendants, was then called, and he said that he and the plaintiff were called "The Brothers Eugene," but the little fellow added confidentially to the Judge, "You know, we are not really brothers, but it is customary in out profession to have those names." The witness had a share in the trapeze, but not in the pole or fittings.

His Honour – And pray how did you become a performer? Witness – I have been a performer about three years, and I began by putting up a pole in the garden.

His Honour – And I suppose you liked it too? Witness – Oh, yes. I am very fond of it. (Laughter) William (the plaintiff) taught me and brought me out.

Plaintiff then informed the court that the detention of the pole was somewhat serious, as he could perform more easily on his old pole, to which he was accustomed, than on a new one.

His Honour thought that was only reasonable. He ruled that as plaintiff had performed for the week, he was entitled to be paid for it, and if he broke his engagement defendants could sue him for damages. The verdict would be for the plaintiff for the salary and damages, less the value of the trapeze, unless the pole and other things were given up within a week.

Verdict for the plaintiff, with costs.

17/3/1867

HISSING IN THEATRES.
A case in some degree affecting the liberty of the subject has just transpired in Sunderland, and a few remarks thereupon may prove interesting to our readers.

Mr George Barker, a shipbuilder, and Town Councillor for Monkwearmouth, was summoned to the Sunderland Police-court, on Friday the 15th inst., and charged with causing a disturbance in front of the Lyceum Theatre on the preceding Tuesday night. The substance of the charge was that Mr Barker hissed, while everyone else applauded, a "spade dance," given by Mr Paul Denlin. Mr Barker continued to hiss, and made remarks upon the spade dancer, whereupon, by order of Mr Bell, the Manager, the offender was remonstrated with by Policeman Hayson. Unfortunately for Mr Barker's case, he spat in the constable's face, and was immediately ejected. He became demonstrative when outside the Theatre, and was taken to the Police-station. Policeman Hayson said the defendant was "very much the worse for liquor; very tipsy indeed." Sub-inspector Hall followed on the same tack, and stated that, when brought to the station, the defendant was "in liquor and excited, but sober enough to know what he was doing;" and Mr Hornsby, a reporter, deposed that he was "certainly the worse for liquor." Neither Mr Hornsby nor Mr Denlin (who came round after the spade dance) heard the defendant use bad language towards the police.

The whole question evidently turned upon Mr Barker's inebriety, and the gentleman himself would probably admit that one person among "a whole Theatre of others" giving expression of feelings of disapprobation while under the influence of refreshment, renders himself amenable to unpleasant consequences. Under the circumstances of Tuesday night, the 12th inst., Mr Barker's hissing would hardly be taken as the evidence of calm, deliberate opinion. The right to hiss is indisputable, and it is quite possible that a spade dance may not possess a great charm for every member of an audience. Every man has a perfect right to hiss if he chooses so to do, but when venturing to give an opinion adverse to the general sentiment he should be in full possession of his reasoning powers. Mr Ranson, who appeared for Mr Bell, would not say the defendant spat in the policeman's face intentionally. Such a compliment could not be paid by a tempestuous lord or a commoner by accident, and this, perhaps, was, after all, the head and front of Mr Barker's offending. The case terminated in Mr Barker's being fined half-a-crown and costs.
24/3/1867

CLOG-OLOGY, THE LANGUAGE OF THE FEET. – I, THOMAS ROBSON, of "Snape," "Gulliver," and "Robson's" Troupe, now performing at the PRINCESS'S CONCERT HALL, LEEDS, will Dance BEN RAY (who challenges the world) in Pumps, Clogs, and Boots, for the small sum of £25 (my own money). The match can come off at the Sun, Knightsbridge, London, or Gatti's, as we shall be Engaged there at Easter.

TROUPE of PERFORMING GOATS ready to take an Engagement – Theatre, Music Hall or Circus. Address, Signor ANTONIO LUCCA, No. 18, Summer-street, Eyre-street-hill, Leather-lane, Holborn. The Goats are very clever.
31/3/1867

HEWLETT'S PATENT TYRIAN LIQUID HAIR DYE, 5 BURLINGTON ARCADE, PICCADILLY. The only one for changing the Hair to any shade from Auburn to Black in five minutes, without staining the skin.

This Dye, which was so well known to the ancients for changing the hair in a few minutes, has been lost to the world, like the GREEK FIRE, for nearly two thousand years. It was accidentally discovered by some antiquarian travellers in Syria and Tyre, and is now introduced to the notice of the British public.

N.B. – A. HEWLETT is the Sole Proprietor of this valuable Hair Dye. There being many spurious Hair Dyes, Ladies and Gentlemen can be satisfied of the effect of the above – A.H. having opened a room where they can have their Hair Dyed, or they can be attended at their own residences by favouring A.H. with their orders. Price per Bottle, 2s. 6d., 8s., 12s., and £1 1s.
21/4/1867

TO WIDOWERS – A LADY, possessing independent means, without any ties of relationship, wishing for a congenial mind with whom to share the pleasures of a home, is desirous of contracting an alliance with some intellectual gentleman. All communications will be treated with the strictest confidence. Address, K.Y., Poste Restante, St Martin's-le-Grand.

THE GREAT FISH BALLOON. – Mr R. ORTON is prepared to make arrangements for Ascents in his New Fish-shape Balloon, handsomely decorated – 20,000 feet capacity. This new Aerostic Machine will prove a great attraction. Early application should be made to Mr R. Orton, 1, Leamouth-place, Orchard House, Blackwall.
28/4/1867

METAMORPHOSES. – Every Night at Eight. – EGYPTIAN HALL, PICCADILLY. – A New Entertainment, in which are displayed Marvels of Instantaneous Invisibility, Darwinism Demented, Flying Heads, Singing Flowers, Marvellous Transmutations of Plants and Animals into Human Beings, and Startling Transformations in Fairyland. Day Performances Wednesday and Saturday, at Three. Sofa Stalls (numbered and reserved), 5s.; Stalls, 3s.; Area, 2s; Admission, 1s. Box-office open daily from Ten to Five. General Manager, Mr H. MEARING.
2/6/1867

AT the Mansion House last Wednesday a young female, aged twenty, attired in a boy's jacket, trousers, vest, and cap, with a pair of Wellington boots, who gave the name of Jane Dixon, was charged before the Lord Mayor under the following circumstances: –

Police-constable Allmans, 860 City, deposed that on Tuesday night, about twelve o'clock, he was on duty in Bishopsgate-street, when he observed the prisoner sitting on a doorstep, apparently in great distress. He accosted her, and, in reply to his question, she stated that she was very tired and hungry, having walked the streets the whole of Sunday night until he found her, and that she had not eaten anything since Monday morning. She stated that she had no friends or home in London, and eventually she told him that she was a girl and not a boy. On this information he took her to the police-station, where her real sex was ascertained and vouched for by the female searcher.

In reply to questions put to her by the Inspector on duty, she stated that she came from Sunderland in the steamboat in order to seek better employment than she had had in that town. The inspector inquired what had been her occupation, and she replied that she had for the last two years worn male attire and filled the situation of barman and waiter at the Jamaica Tavern in High-street, Sunderland, and she accounted for the fact that her real sex had never been discovered during her two years' service by the circumstance that she had always had a bedroom to herself.

The Lord Mayor, after conferring with Mr Oke, the chief clerk, resolved upon sending the prisoner to the workhouse for the present, to give her time to consider what course she would take with regard to herself, and also to decide upon the best course to be adopted with respect to her. The "female," who seemed deeply ashamed of the position in which the discovery had placed her, was removed from the court, and conveyed to the workhouse by the female searcher.

PIER HOTEL GARDENS, ERITH. – There was an immense gathering of holiday folks at these gardens on Whit Monday. Amusements of extraordinary variety were provided, the fair sex and the rising generation being considered in the arrangements equally with the gentlemen. The feat which created, probably, the greatest amount of interest and merriment was the plucky aquatic performance of Mr W. Gosford, of Knockholt, a hale and hearty gentleman, who has now passed the allotted span of three score and ten years. In accordance with a previous announcement, Mr Gosford seated himself in a common washing tub, which his weight sank almost to the water's level. A splendid team of ganders were got into harness, and no sooner had the venerable Captain grasped the ribbons than the geese dashed off in grand style. Among other performances, a remarkably sagacious and highly-trained dog ran up and down upon his hind legs while a cat, nearly as big as himself, hung round his neck. Upon the whole, what with dancing and kissing in the ring, and the inevitable concomitant of flirting, the Pier Hotel probably never had a gayer time of it than on Monday last.
16/6/1867

A Paper Life-Buoy.
Mr Johnson, a comedian, of Douglas's dramatic company, has been for some time exerting his very ingenious mind, and in his leisure time has constructed a life-buoy made of paper, which, being but five feet long, and *weighing only ten pounds*, is considered of sufficient buoyancy to save two or three persons from drowning. In shape it is like a huge cigar, with two taper ends, having on each side a

wooden rod, attached to the cone by bands of light iron. The balance is effected by two three-inch tin tubes affixed to the bottom. On Wednesday the novel invention was launched on the Grantham and Nottingham Canal, and in its trial, as far as buoyancy was concerned, fully answered expectations, the efforts of the men to submerge it being fruitless. The counter-balance was not quite so happy, being insufficient when the rod was clutched on one side, but this can be remedied by altering the shape of the tubes. Altogether, this, the first, trial was most successful, Mr Johnson being complimented by Sir John Lawson and all present on the efficiency of his simple but most useful invention.

We know not to whom Mr Johnson intends to offer his life-buoy, but, from observation, should certainly say that the purpose for which it is most adapted is for saving life *in case of accident on the ice*. We have seen cases where the buoy or barrow now in use has by its weight broken in the ice before it could reach the person in the water. Now, this paper life-buoy, with a pair of skates attached to the tubes at the bottom (weighing, as it does, but ten pounds) might be sent almost any distance, with greater speed, greater safety, and answer the same purpose, beside being made at a very small cost.
23/6/1867

DANCING for the STAGE and BALL ROOM. – M. ST. MAINE (of the THEATRES ROYAL, DRURY-LANE and COVENT-GARDEN), begs to announce his newly-built Dancing Academy, ALEXANDRA VILLA, BIRKBECK-ROAD, HORNSEY-RISE. Private Lessons Day or Evening. Young Ladies prepared for the Ballet or Principal Dancers. Young Gentlemen taught to Play Harlequin or Clown; a thorough knowledge of the business, dances, &c., guaranteed. Engagements procured. Sailors' Hornpipes, Highland Flings, Clog Hornpipes, Break-downs, Jigs, and every description of Burlesque Dances. Private instruction till perfect in each dance, £1 1s. Articled Pupils taken for Three Years. Ladies and Gentlemen can be made perfect in all Ball Room Dancing in a few easy private lessons.
30/6/1867

BATHING WITHOUT DRAWERS AT RAMSGATE. – The Rev. J.S. Jones was charged with bathing without drawers on the 2nd inst. P.C. Hitter stated that he saw the defendant and two other gentlemen bathing without drawers, and waited until the machine came to the sands, and when he told them of the offence the defendant had committed he said he had forgotten to put the drawers on. The defendant pleaded guilty, and was fined 2. 6d. and 9s. costs.
14/7/1867

THE WONDERFUL FAIRY SINGING BIRDS FOR SALE. – These Two Extraordinary Mechanical Birds are only the size of Butterflies, one a Nightingale, the other a Bullfinch. They sing for half an hour all the sweet and delicious notes of the above beautiful birds, the graceful movements of their head, beak, wings, and tail being the same as in the living bird. They surpass in every way the Piping Bullfinch. The birds sing in two small golden cages, which are erected in a very handsome Golden Temple, forming the greatest wonders ever seen or heard in Europe. To be seen at Mr Bland's Magical Repository, 478, New Oxford-street, opposite Mudie's Library.

ATTEMPT TO BLOW UP EXETER THEATRE. – About ten o'clock on Thursday night (11th inst.) a light was perceived in the Exeter Theatre. Before dark the building had been safely locked up, and the keys placed in the custody of the usual parties, and as it was known that no-one could have business in the Theatre at that hour, there being no performance on Thursday night, Mr Nelson, Acting Manager, and Mr Barker, who is connected with the Bristol Company, who had been performing at Exeter, were communicated with. They, accompanied by some friends, entered the building by the front door, and on going into the body of the Theatre found a small jet burning, but perceived, both by smell and hearing, that there was a serious escape of gas. Further search showed that the main pipes had been unscrewed, and gas was seen issuing from it with tremendous force. After stopping the escape, search was made for the perpetrator of the villainous act, but no-one could be found on the premises. Had not the light been observed, it is inevitable that a great explosion would have taken place, and probably the Theatre would have been burned down. The guilty person must have entered the premises by means of a skeleton key, and must have been well acquainted with the arrangement of the building, and the position of the gas meter. The properties of the Bristol company were in the Theatre packed ready for removal.

On Monday Walter Graham (son of the late Mrs Bolton) was placed at the bar of the Exeter Guildhall, being charged with the above offence, when sufficient evidence was brought against him to remand him until Wednesday, when, after a lengthened examination, the Bench retired for consultation for a few minutes, and on returning into court the Chairman asked the prisoner if he had anything to say in answer to the charge. Prisoner – I have nothing to say. The Chairman – The Bench think it is a case of such grave suspicion that it had better be investigated before a Jury; and they, therefore, commit the prisoner for trial at the next Assizes. Prisoner was then remanded in custody. The case occupied the court four hours and a half.

NORTH RIDING ASYLUM, CLIFTON, YORK. WANTED, immediately, a Good Under GARDEN ATTENDANT. Salary to commence at £25 per annum, with Board, Lodging, and Washing. One that can Play in a Brass Band will be preferred. Apply to Dr CHRISTIE, Medical Superintendent.
21/7/1867

LORD ARTHUR CLINTON. – "BUSKIN," in *The Times* of Tuesday, commented on the seeming impropriety of the advertisements announcing Lord Arthur Pelham Clinton's nightly appearance in a screaming farce at the Holborn Theatre, at a time when his uncle, the late Lord Robert Clinton, was lying unburied at Clumber. Messrs Scoles, Hanrott, and Pain, of 44, Bedford-row, Lord Arthur's solicitors, at once forwarded to *The Times* a copy of a placard posted both in and outside the Holborn Theatre on Friday, the 26th ult.: "In consequence of a domestic bereavement, Lord Arthur Pelham Clinton is unable to appear this evening. The indulgence of the audience is, therefore, respectfully solicited for those gentlemen who have taken his parts at so short a notice." [Mr "Buskin" should have ascertained particulars before he committed his false ideas to paper.]

KLEO'S BLOOM of LILIES imparts a permanent Whiteness to the Skin. Specially recommended to Actresses. By post, Eight Stamps. J. GRIFFITH and Co., 13, Lamb's Conduit-street, London, W.C.
4/8/1867

THE PERFORMING SEAL AND ITS KEEPER. – Frederick Churcher, a youth, giving his place of abode as a common lodging-house, was charged before Mr Traill, last Monday, at the Greenwich Police-court, with obtaining a bag containing wearing apparel, value £3, under false pretences, the property of William Wall. Richard Mallett, manager of a lodging-house at Deptford, produced a note purported to be written and signed by the prosecutor, and which was presented by the prisoner, requiring the property named in the charge to be delivered to the bearer. The prosecutor, a seafaring man, said he was travelling the country with a performing seal, and having met with an accident in the Old Kent Road, the prisoner and his father were recommended to him, and he engaged their services. After sleeping at a lodging-house at Deptford, where he left his clothes, he went to Ramsgate, and on returning he found that his clothes had been obtained by the prisoner on the order presented to the last witness.

Mr Traill (to the prosecutor) – What are you? Prosecutor – A traveller with the performing seal, a monster of the deep. (Laughter.) Mr Traill – Then you are the keeper of the seal? Prosecutor – Partly so, your Worship, although the seal has kept me. (Renewed laughter.) Mr Traill – A performing seal – I suppose it is a human being who is the real performing seal? Prosecutor – No, your Worship, a real monster from the ocean. (Laughter.) Mr Traill – And of what does its performance consist? Prosecutor – At a given signal it will get out of the water, ascend a platform, sound the tambourine, and play the triangle. (Loud laughter.) Mr Traill – My advice to you is, to keep to your seafaring life, and not travel the country with any such exhibition.

The prisoner, in answer to the Magistrate, said he was sent by his father with the note and obtained the prosecutor's bag, which he gave to his father, of whose whereabouts he was not now aware. Mr Traill remanded the prisoner.
29/9/1867

ELOPEMENT OF PROFESSIONAL SISTERS. – Not the least active equestriennes of the troupe of Mr Newsome, Circus Proprietor, now in Blackburn, were his two daughters, the Misses Adele and Emma, both daring and accomplished riders. Last week these young ladies accomplished a flight which must even have greatly astonished their papa – they both eloped, the one with a Mr Meers, and the other with a Mr Coleman, who was also amongst that gentleman's company. It has since transpired that the runaway lovers were married in Manchester on the morning of their escape. Rumour statesd that one of the ladies leaves at once for India, where her husband has an engagement.

HUBERT MEERS, Champion Somersault Thrower on Horseback, and England's only Flying Trapeze Artist; also Mrs Hubert Meers (late Miss Adele Newsome), the First Female Equestrian of the age, having made arrangements with a Mr John Wilson to join his great World Circus in Bombay, will leave England in a few days. H.M. would like to hear from his Father immediately. Address, HUBERT MEERS, 4, Mortimer-street, London.

Paris! Paris! Paris! FRED BEVAN. – Another Immense Success, and Re-engagement of the Great Clown and Musical Grotesque at the GRAND AMERICAN CIRQUE and CIRQUE IMPERIAL. FRED BEVAN and his WOODEN-HEADED FAMILY. – The beauty of the clever Acrobatic Troupe is there is not the slightest danger to unnerve the most nervous person who may frequent such amusement. The Boys are perfectly safe under their Papa's care. No black looks at the Boys, or sly pinches. They amuse old and young, rich and poor.
N.B. – Acrobatic fathers, be kind to your Kids.

TO PROPRIETORS OF ENTERTAINMENTS AND OTHERS. TO BE SOLD, a Bargain, a Mechanical Exhibition of THE SIEGE AND FALL OF SEBASTAPOL, quite New, and superior to anything of the kind yet exhibited, with innumerable Working Figures, and Shipping of English and French Fleets, Scenery, Drapery, Gas Fittings, &c., all complete; to which is added a Beautiful Representation of "The Eruption of Mount Vesuvius," with Moving Figures, Boats, &c. Address, post paid, A.Y., 32, Cook-street, near Waterloo-street, Camberwell, London.
13/10/1867

TO THE MANAGERS OF GREAT PANTOMIMES, &c.
GREAT STAR TROUP OF BEDOUIN ARABS (Twelve in Number), from Cabeil. This Extraordinary Tribe – Children of the Desert – the most wonderful company of performers that ever visited England – all fine men, picked athletes – may justly be termed the Stars of the Sahara. Can challenge the world in their Great Leaping Act over Men and Horses, Tourbilions, Pyramids, &c., &c.
MAHOMED BEN CHERZ (*Directeur de la Troupe*, from Cabeil),
HADJ-ALLASON (The Lion Leaper of Forty-three Feet, on the Ground),
MOLAH-AMBARK (The Tiger Leaper of the Desert),
BEL HUSAN (The Crocodile),
HADJ-ANNASAC (The Python),
HADJ-BRIAN (The Dagger Leaper),
ABDALAH (The Whirlwind),

ALI-ABDALAH (The Mountain Cat, from the Atlas Mountains),
HADJ-ASAHAZ (The Rhinoceros),
TILLY-BEN-MAHOMED (*Le Serpent du Desert*),
SIDI-BETEL-CADOUR (The Dragon Fly),
BEN HUDAH (*El Ombra Elephant* – carries the whole troupe on his shoulders).

All applications as to engagements, vacant dates, &c., to be made to Mr VAN HARE (the Original), at his Town Residence, 64, Stafford-place, Buckingham Palace.

TO MUSICAL PROFESSIONALS, or those who wish to be Musical in a very Short Time – LISKARD'S CHROMATIC TEA-POT, handsomely finished in Metal, from £2 10s.; in Silver, from £15 10s. To be had of C. COULE, Importer of Musical Instruments, 37, St Martin's-lane, Charing-cross.
20/10/1867

THE FATAL ACCIDENT TO MRS MAY.
ON Thursday Mr Richards, the Deputy Coroner for Middlesex, held an inquiry at the Queen's Head Tavern, Green Lanes, Tottenham, respecting the death of Mrs Mary Anne May, aged forty years.

Mr Samuel May, the well-known theatrical costumier, of Bow-street, said that the deceased was his wife. She lived at his private residence, at St. John's Villa, West Green, Tottenham. For the last twenty-one years she had been afflicted with epileptic fits. They were more periodical at the turn of the moon, and she became weak in intellect. She would sit silent for a length of time, and she would not enter into conversation with any person. She was carefully watched, and for fear of an accident taking place, he had fire-guards put up in front of all the fire-grates of the house.

Miss Mary Louisa May, a young lady who was quite overcome by grief, said that the deceased was her mother. On Tuesday morning, at twenty minutes to ten o'clock, she was seated with her in the dining room. The deceased was close to the fire. There was a guard on the grate. Witness left the room for a moment to get a cup of coffee, and while she was away she heard a heavy fall upon the floor. She ran back and found the deceased lying on the floor and her clothes were all in flames. Her head and neck were dreadfully burnt. Witness ran out of the room into the garden and told a gentleman what had happened, and he then went to her mother's assistance.

By the Coroner – Last summer her mother had a similar fall, and she then cut her eye.

Mr Alexander Robins, a gentleman who lives next door to Mr May's house at St. John's Villa, said – On Tuesday I heard a cry of "Fire!"

The Coroner – Were you called in?

Witness – Miss May ran out into the garden and cried out, "Mrs May is on fire!" and I then entered the house, where I saw the deceased lying on the hearthrug, in the dining room. She was all in flames. I suppose her daughter had pulled her away from the fire-grate. She was quite dead, and I applied cold water to extinguish the fire. The fire-guard had been removed from the front of the fire-place, and a poker was lying underneath her. I think she had removed the guard to poke the fire while Miss May was out of the room, and that she fell on the bars of the grate while she was in the act of doing so.

Mr William T. Watson, M.R.C.S., said that he was called in to the deceased on Tuesday at a quarter to ten o'clock.

The Coroner – You must have been there immediately, and the whole occurrence must have taken place in a very short time.

Witness – Yes; I think her death must have taken place almost at once. She was dreadfully burnt; her face was carbonised. There was a mark across her forehead and her face, caused by the fall across the hot bars of the grate. Her death was caused by suffocation and by shock to the system, arising from the severe nature of the burns she had received.

The Coroner said that the case was a very painful one. He did not think that the deceased had had any intention of destroying her life when she removed the guard. No doubt, while she was poking the fire, she was seized with a fit, and fell on the bars. He must say that Mr May had taken every precaution to prevent the occurrence, which appeared to have been a pure accident.

The Jury returned a verdict, "That the deceased was found dead from the mortal effects of burns, and that such burns were caused accidentally."

MADAME TUSSAUD'S. – Life-size portrait models of Victor Emmanuel, King of Italy, and Garibaldi are now to be seen at the Historical Gallery, Baker-street. The likenesses are most striking. Now that the brave old General is incarcerated within the walls of an Italian fortress, we feel assured that every admirer of that gallant soldier will be interested when visiting Madame Tussaud's Exhibition.

PANTOMIME TRICKS. – The Best Trick to introduce is the Bowls of Water and Gold Fish from an Empty Scarf, and Bowls of Liquid Fire, which, upon being touched, burst into a volume of flame. Price, large size, 7s. each; small, 5s.; of A. TAYLOR, Magical Apparatus Maker, Seven Sisters' Cottage, Holloway, London, N.
10/11/1867

"CASTE."
TO THE EDITOR OF THE ERA.
Sir, – Will you have the kindness to publish the enclosed correspondence? Your obedient servant, T.W. ROBERTSON. London, Nov. 26th, 1867.

To Mr Lester Wallack, Wallack's Theatre, New York. Sept. 6th, 1867.
Dear Mr Wallack, – I am sorry to trouble you again about the piracy of *Caste*, but I have just received a letter from Mr Florence, so audacious, and, at the same time, so humorous, that I cannot withhold it from the public. Here it is:

Broadway Theatre, Manager's Office, Aug. 20th, 1867.
T.W. Robertson, Esq. – My dear Sir, – When in London this summer in search of novelties, I had the pleasure of seeing your admirable comedy of *Caste*, and was so much pleased with it that I witnessed it several times, *and from memory drafted a copy*, as near as possible, *for the American market*. Feeling from the existing laws between the two countries (there being no international copyright) *I had as much right to play it as any other party*, I produced it with great success; and to prove to you that I was right, the case was tested, and I enclose you the decision of the Supreme (our highest) Court. *But I am, too just a man to benefit by the labour of another without sharing that benefit with him*. Under the circumstances, I send you a draft for £50, *not as a matter of right, but one of fairness between man and man*. Trusting you will receive it with the same spirit in which it is sent, and hoping, also, that I may be able to induce you to write a drama for me on your own terms, permit me to remain, your obedient servant, W.J. FLORENCE.

To this effusion I returned the following reply:

London, Sept. 6th, 1867
Sir, – I have to acknowledge the receipt of a letter from you enclosing me a cheque for £50. I refuse to accept the £50, which I return to you through the hands of Mr Lester Wallack; and I wish you to understand that now, and for the future, I refuse to hold any communication with you. I am, Sir, your obedient servant, T.W. ROBERTSON.

I should tell you, my dear Mr Wallack, that I know nothing whatever of Mr Florence, except that, some years ago, I saw a man of that name act very badly at the Princess's Theatre; and that this summer I received a letter from a Mr Florence asking me to write a piece for him. With a vivid recollection of the performance at the Princess's, I told him, with perfect truth, that I had accepted engagements for some months. Let me here say that the person I saw at the Princess's Theatre may not have been the same Mr Florence whose wonderful powers of memory have -------- you and and me of so much money.

My motive in sending back to Mr Florence the £50 through you is obvious – the return of the money cannot be denied. Mr Florence must understand that I am not a receiver of stolen goods, particularly when the property purloined happens to have been taken from my own house. There is, besides, a poetical injustice in his getting back his little offer of "hush money" from the hands of the man he has so much injured, which he is, doubtless, "too just a man" to comprehend.

Let me once more express my regret at your loss in this matter. Mr Florence cannot, of course, understand that robbery is robbery, even though the theft can be committed with impunity; but here he may reckon without his host. Although the law has decided against us, public opinion in America is in our favour, and Mr Florence will find public opinion a dangerous thing to brave. To the American public, therefore, I confidently leave his punishment.

After all, persons of Mr Florence's kind may be useful in their way. The case decided against us may be a small step towards a much-needed law of International Copyright*, and to that good end Mr Florence has been a soiled and humble instrument.

I am, dear Mr Wallack, yours very faithfully, T.W. ROBERTSON.

*The International Copyright Act was not passed until 1891.

SINGULAR ACCIDENT TO AN ACTRESS. – A few nights since at Greenock, while Miss Adelaide Ross was performing the part of Juliet, in Shakespeare's play of *Romeo and Juliet*, and towards the close of the last act, where the actress is supposed to stab herself, the weapon used upon the occasion being a very sharp-pointed one, Miss Ross actually caused the dagger to pierce her flesh immediately over the region of the heart. The curtain thereafter fell, when it was ascertained that blood was coming from the wound. Upon examination it was found that the weapon, having fortunately pierced the actress in oblique direction, had escaped touching a vital part, and the injury was not so severe as to prevent Miss Ross appearing on the following evening.

1/12/1867

TOTAL DESTRUCTION OF HER MAJESTY'S THEATRE.
LAST night (Friday, Dec. 6th, 1867), at five minutes to eleven o'clock, an alarm was raised in the Haymarket that Her Majesty's Theatre was on fire, which unfortunately proved to be correct, as flames were seen in a few minutes rushing from the windows of the upper part of the building.

Before half-past eleven the fire had a terrific hold of the Theatre, and threatened destruction to all the block of houses around it in Pall-Mall, Haymarket, Charles-street, and Regent-street. The Theatre burnt like tinder, and the Cigar Warehouse of Mr Brumfit, as well as Messrs Leader, soon fell a prey to the flames.

The sight from the Saloon Balcony of the Haymarket Theatre was a scene not to be forgotten by those who witnessed it, every inch of pavement and road being occupied by thousands of persons. The church of St Mary's, Strand, was so distinctly lighted that anyone, even at a reasonable distance, could see the time by the clock, and the Charing-cross Hotel will never, we hope, look so brilliant from any similar cause. The noble church of St Martin's was seen in all its architectural beauty, and the heat from the flames was uncomfortably felt on the steps.

At the time we write the building is still blazing, and there is no prospect of the conflagration being extinguished for some hours.

The Theatre, at the time of its destruction, was under the Lesseeship of Mr Mapleson with an autumn season of Italian Opera, but last night (Friday) no performance took place. On Thursday *Il Don Giovanni* was represented, with Tietjens, Kellogg, Sinico, Santley, Hohler, Zobodi, and Foli in the cast, and Mozart's *chef d'oevre* proved to be the last opera performed in the ill-fated building.

8/12/1867

FATAL TRAPEZE ACCIDENT. – On Friday (6th inst.) an inquest was held at St Bartholomew's Hospital by Mr W.J. Payne, Deputy-Coroner, relative to the death of Phillip Milton, aged twenty-five years. The deceased was a carpenter living at 45, Murry-street, Hoxton, and he erected a trapeze in the back yard for himself and another to practice on. While swinging one day with his feet through two iron rings and his head hanging downwards he slipped, and fell heavily to the ground. His spine was broken, and he was taken to the hospital, where he lingered for several days. He died on Tuesday last. It appeared that the deceased had only practiced gymnastics for a month, and the manoeuvre which cost him his life was the first of the kind which he tried, although it is generally the last which people are permitted to attempt at regular gymnasiums. The Jury returned a verdict of "Accidental death."

THE BILL POSTERS OF HUDDERSFIELD. – To Proprietors of Entertainments and their Agents in Advance. In order that the above Parties may not be deceived or led astray when visiting the town of Huddersfield, the Bill Posters hereby intimate that ALL the POSTING PLACES in the Town (except four) have been LEASED or RENTED by the said Bill Posters conjointly, and that Posting on said Walls, &c., is their exclusive right.
15/12/1867

9
1868
ONE HIDEOUS JUMBLE

AMATEUR THEATRICALS AT ALDERSHOT CAMP.
TO THE EDITOR OF THE ERA.
Sir, – As we have incurred considerable unmerited censure by reason of the dresses and appointments, arranged to be supplied by us to the noblemen and gentlemen who took part in the performance at Aldershot on the 7th of December last, not having arrived at their destination in time, and thereby causing considerable inconvenience, and disappointment to our patrons and to the large and distinguished audience assembled to witness the performance on that evening, we beg to say that we have consented to accept, and have received, from the South-Western Railway the sum of £10, as an acknowledgment of their negligence in delaying the delivery of the cases containing the dresses and appointments; and which were duly intrusted to the company's care by us for delivery at the Aldershot railway station. We trust you will favour us by inserting this letter, that as far as possible our numerous and distinguished patrons who honoured the representation may know that the railway company and not ourselves is the cause of the disappointment. We are, Sir, your obedient servants, LEWIS and HENRY NATHAN.
5/1/1868

MECHANICAL HEAD FOR SALE, Twelve Feet High, Seventeen Wide, well made of good material; Mechanism perfect, an excellent Comic Scene, a Novelty for a Music Hall. For particulars, apply to Mr THOMAS JACKSON, Royal Pavilion, Sheffield.
12/1/1868

THE POET AND THE PORT WINE.
AT the Marylebone County Court, on Wednesday, Mr Page, Italian warehouseman, of Westbourne-grove, sued Mr Robert Browning, the poet, for 8s., the value of two bottles of port wine.
   Plaintiff said that formerly defendant was a customer, but not giving enough perquisites to the housekeeper the custom was taken away. A lad called on the 8th July last and said Mr Browning wished two bottles of port wine, and as he (plaintiff) had previously known the lad to be in defendant's service, he let him have the wine on credit.
   Mr Browning, in defence, said he had not dealt with plaintiff for two years. He never drank port wine, nor did anyone else in the house. He never ordered it from anyone. On the 8th of July, when the bottles were alleged to have been given to his page, that lad had been in his service for six months. He was shown to plaintiff at the time of his making his demand, and he then shuffled in his statement, and said it was another lad who had called. Mr Browning concluded an indignant speech by calling his housekeeper and page, both of whom deposed they had never ordered or received port wine from plaintiff or anybody else for Mr Browning's house.

His Honour (Mr Jessell) said plaintiff had not shown a proper amount of caution in his dealings and judgement would be given for defendant.

Mr Browning said he had lost the whole day in connection with this paltry claim, but he resisted it on principle. He wished his costs to be appropriated to the poor-box of the court, for which he was publicly thanked by the Registrar.

ENDANGERING THE LIFE OF A CLOWN.

A CASE which formed the theme of considerable excitement was brought before the Magistrates at the Sunderland Police-court, on the 9th inst., in which two men, named respectively Thomas Purse and Henry Brown, recently employed as scene-shifters at the Lyceum Theatre, Sunderland, stood charged with having committed a breach of contract by refusing to perform one of the duties assigned to them. Mr Clarence Holt, Lessee of the above-named place of amusement, attended the court in the expectation that the defendants would acknowledge their guilt, in the event of which he would simply have asked that they might be reprimanded by the Magistrates, but the men, under the instructions of Mr Robson, who appeared for them, declined to enter that plea, on account of which the case was fully entered into. […] The facts, as made plain by the evidence, were these:

On the evening of the 24th of December the defendants, who were appointed to stand behind one of the scenes for the purpose of receiving into their theatrical embrace the transformed body of Prince Hasanrac (Mr Hudspeth, the Clown) in one of the comic scenes of the Pantomime, known as *Ali Baba*, made up their minds to desert their posts when they ought to be waiting at the back of "the looking-glass," through which the bounding man of fun and frolic has to jump for the amusement of the audience. It appears that there was a conspiracy amongst certain persons engaged there to oppose the performance of this service, on the ground that Mr Hudspeth had not "shelled out" what is known as catch-money for drink, as was desired. One of the defendants (Brown) was set aside, and the case of Purse only was taken, the latter admitting that he had been prompted by some of the carpenters to return a shilling which Mr Hudspeth had given, although 10s. had been promised for the benefit night. The Clown had told the men that Mr Holt paid them for their services, which ought to be sufficient.

It had been whispered to Mr Hudspeth in the course of the day that he had better keep his weather eye open, or he would meet with an accident, on account of which watch and ward were kept by Mr Holt on the occasion of the fifth catch, which went off without accident; but on his being absent the second time the men left their places, and had it not been for Mr Garden and Mr Holt, Jun., who ran to the rescue, the merry countenance of the Clown would have suffered a transformation that all the Fairy Queens in Pantomimes could not have reversed – in other words, he would, in taking what is known as the "lion's leap," have pitched his head against a back wall, after jumping a distance of five feet, and probably have fallen down a trap of ten or twelve feet in depth. Notwithstanding Mr Holt's remonstrances and complaints, the defendants, who had been discharged from the premises, went on the following Saturday to demand their wages, but were refused. Evidence respecting the above facts was given by Mr Holt, Mr Hodges, and Mr Garden.

A long dispute followed, in which Mr Robson contended that the men were not handicraftsmen as implied in the Masters and Servants Act, which was passed in the reign of Queen Elizabeth, when players were looked upon as rogues and vagabonds, and were not deemed to be labourers or artisans. He argued that these men were employed to attend upon and assist the performers, and although they did not appear in front of the curtain, their labour being essential to the completeness of the Pantomime, they were performers, and not handicraftsmen, the latter of which he interpreted to mean one who constructed or produced any article.

Mr Bell, on the other hand, argued that, as the men were employed to work the machinery of the Theatre, and to be at the bidding of the Manager within given hours, for which they were paid a weekly salary, and as they were engaged by the chief carpenter, and worked in conjunction with him, they were "employed in manual labour," and such was Walker's definition of a handicraftsman. They were, therfore, amenable to the law. [...]

The Magistrates informed Mr Bell that as he had not produced the head carpenter, who had made the contract with the defendant, they were bound to accept the statement of the latter, which was to the effect that he was engaged to shift scenes and *nothing else*. Had that contract been proved it is exceedingly probable that the defendant would have been sent to prison without the option of paying a fine. It was due to Mr Holt, and to all persons employed under him, that he should have a public inquiry into the case.

Mr Harley added that the defendant's conduct had been exceedingly bad, and it would have been more becoming if he had expressed his sorrow for his conduct.

Mr Bell concurred with the decision of the Bench, and said that he never expected to have proceeded with the case, believing that both defendants would express their contrition. He should, however, take out a fresh summons against Brown.

19/1/1868

FATAL ACCIDENT AT A THEATRE. – A sad and fatal accident has occurred at the Theatre Royal, Leicester. It seems, from the evidence adduced at the inquest, held on Tuesday evening before the Coroner, Mr J. Gregory, that on Saturday night at the Theatre, which is now under the Management of Mr G.H. Ashton, was extremely full, and that the deceased, Henry Payne, a youth about twelve years of age, at his own request, accompanied his father into the gallery for the purpose of witnessing the performance of the Pantomime, *Little Red Riding Hood*. In the course of the entertainment, owing to the crowded state of the gallery, the deceased and about thirty others were let into the "side slips" adjoining, and while there, looking over the front on to the stage, it would seem that some mischievous youths succeeded in carrying unperceived into the gallery, from the lobby, a large and heavy door for the purpose of making a platform from which to obtain a better view of the performance, but which overpowered them and fell with considerable force on to the back of the deceased, crushing him severely against the front of the gallery, and causing him to sustain severe internal injuries, from which he died on Tuesday. The Jury returned a verdict of "Accidental death," and Mr Ashton promised to secure the door, and to pay the funeral expenses of the unfortunate youth.

TO DOG MEN AND DUOLOGUE ARTISTS. – CHARLIE MELTON wishes to DISPOSE OF his Highly-Trained NEWFOUNDLAND DOG, CORA. In good condition and beautifully marked Black and White. C.M. having been rendered destitute by long illness, and now in an advanced stage of consumption, would be glad of any trifling assistance from his Friends. Address, Norfolk Ward, Consumptive Hospital, Brompton.

26/1/1868

THE RIVAL BARBERS. – Nelson Towell, a hairdresser, living at No. 15, Parson's-street, Kingsland-road, was placed at the bar of Guildhall Police-court, on remand, before Alderman Lusk, M.P., charged with having committed a violent assault on John Carson, another hairdresser, at 207, Upper Whitecross-street. Mr Carson said that he had the privilege of going daily into Whitecross-street Prison, to attend on the prisoners; but, the defendant having nothing to do, he allowed him to go in and take the work. He had had it about two years, but latterly got very negligent, and did not go to the prison for days together. He (complainant) was, consequently, obliged to go himself.

On Thursday morning, when he came out of the prison, the prisoner came up to him, and, using bad language, said, "You are a pretty fellow." Witness said, "What for?" and, without any explanation, he said, "Take that," and struck him a blow in the right eye, which cut his eyelid and blackened his eye. In reply to questions put by the prisoner, prosecutor said he did not make a dart at him while he was crossing the road, but he (prisoner) said, "Carson, you are a ------ shabby fellow to go and undermine me." Thomas Wright, 28, New College-row, Tooley-street, said he saw the prisoner strike the complainant, and while he was looking for a policeman to give him into custody the prisoner said, "If you are a man put up your hands and hit me back again." The prisoner was so tipsy that Alderman Lusk remanded him till he was sober. He now said, in defence, that Carson made the first blow at him, and that he only struck in self-defence. This was denied by both the witnesses. Mr Alderman Lusk fined the prisoner 40s., or, in default, fourteen days imprisonment with hard labour.

GREAT CURIOSITY. – FOR SALE, ALIVE, a RED PIG, with SIX LEGS. Apply at 70, Vauxhall Walk, Lambeth.
2/2/1868

A SPECTACLE NOT SET DOWN IN THE BILL. – A few evenings since there was a performance at the Worcester Theatre of the opera *Rob Roy*. In the last act a Scotch reel had to be danced. The Manager and his leader of the orchestra had not been on good terms, and on the evening in question their disagreement rose to a climax. The music to the dance was played so strangely as to draw down hisses from the audience, and dreadfully bother the performers. The Manager interfered, and stated to the hissing audience that one of the company should play the dance music instead. This was done, and the reel at last satisfactorily reeled through. Shortly afterwards the leader, having occasion to go upon the stage to perform a violin solo, took an opportunity, against all theatrical rule and propriety, to break out into an address to the audience. This was too much, and Mr McFadyen, the Manager, bolting on to the stage, collared the oratorical delinquent with intent to lead or drag him off, but he would not consent to be so easily removed from before the footlights, and a smart pummelling and cuffing match was enacted, to the infinite delight of the audience, who manifested the interest they took in the game of fisticuffs by uproarious shouts and cheers. At last the Manager succeeded in dragging his refractory subordinate from the stage, and the pair disappeared at one of the wings. Shortly after, however, the fiddler reappeared in his place in the orchestra, but here he was soon revisited by the wrathful Manager, who, with the aid of a policeman, removed him, and finally thrust him off the premises.

THE ART OF ADVERTISING. – Ordinary handbills now look as smart as a rainbow, and street hoardings, when pasted over, stand as gay as Harlequins. The literature of the walls is a pleasing sight and study, evincing great progress in typography, and showing the commercial energy of the age. The strolling bill-sticker is an historical being, whose place is filled by the contracting bill-poster, with his wagon and mechanism. A new mode of gaining publicity is now offered to go-a-head people in "Bell's Magic Transparent Advertising Cards," beautifully printed in chromo, which are really a novelty, extremely simple, highly attractive, and supremely effective, the one attribute that must ensure their adoption by Lessees of Theatres, Managers of Public Entertainments, and all pushing firms. As evidence of their effectiveness many hundred persons may be daily seen at the Crystal Palace, the Polytechnic, on London-bridge, and other places, much amused with these cards, and, after holding them up to the light – thus reading their mystery – carefully pocket them for future service amongst their friends, every card thus obtaining numberless readers. Mr George Bell may be congratulated on his clever "hit" and its certain success.
9/2/1868

LITTLE RED RIDING HOOD'S FAREWELL TO HER JUVENILE FRIENDS.
"Good-bye, dears, and thank you very much for your kind visits to me. The cruel Wolf tried very hard to entrap me, but my dear Jack Horner has given him so severe a lesson that I am sure he will not trouble us any more. Froggy (poor, silly Froggy) has gone back to his Mother, and, safe below in the depths of the Green Pond, he promises ne'er again to go a-wooing without her consent; indeed, I hear he has joined the Bulrush Volunteers (uniform, a bright yellow, turned up with green). I and Jack are to be

married as soon as the buttercups and daisies come in, and as Granny has left me her rose-covered cottage – dear Jack will be able to farm the land there in peace and contentment – we hope to be happy all the rest of our lives. Jacky says I must never leave off my cloak, for he loves it as part of myself; so you see, although I shall soon become his bride, I shall always be

Yours truly, dears, with many thanks,

"LITTLE RED RIDING HOOD."

"P.S. – Wolf has just written to say that he is very sorry he ate dear Grandmother, but I don't think I can ever forgive him, for all we have found of the poor, dear old lady has been her spectacles."

16/2/1868

What is Being in "Character?"

A CASE of considerable importance was heard at the County Court, Bolton, on the 14th inst., before J.S.T. Greene, Esq., County Court Judge, in which Mr Harry West, comic singer, was the plaintiff, and Mr John Smith, Proprietor of the Star Inn Concert Room, the defendant.

The plaintiff and his wife (Polly Charlton) had been engaged at Mr Smith's establishment from the 30th of December last to the 25th January. Plaintiff was engaged as a "comic character vocalist," and his wife as a "character vocalist and dancer." From the evidence of defendant and several other witnesses, it appeared that for the first two weeks of their engagement they both appeared in "character"; but in the third week, an unpleasantness having taken place, they did not dress in "character," and on another occasion Mr West was not ready to appear when the bell rang. The rules of the establishment, which had been signed by the plaintiff, imposed a fine of sixpence for not being ready for the stage when the bell rang, and also a fine of sixpence for not appearing in character, and for infringement of these rules plaintiff was fined 14s. 6d. the third week, and 20s. in the fourth week, those amounts having been deducted from his salary.

Plaintiff alleged that he always appeared in "character," as did also his wife. Plaintiff always sang swell songs, for which he changed his hat and wore a "sensation" coat.

His Honour – Does one "sensation" coat do for all the swell songs? Plaintiff said he changed his dress. Mrs West always appeared in character, with a short dress on.

His Honour – If she appeared with a short dress on, would not she be out of character?

Plaintiff called several witnesses to prove that both he and his wife always appeared in some character or other.

His Honour – Yes; but if they sang a sailor's song, and appeared as the Grand Seigneur, that would not be a proper character. He understood the character dress should be suitable for the character represented.

The witness for the defence proved that, during the first two weeks, Mrs West changed her dresses to suit the dances or songs she represented. If a sailor's dance she was in a sailor's costume, whereas, on the third and fourth weeks, she wore one dress the whole evening for all her songs and dances, and that Mr West appeared sometimes in his street coat, the one he had on in court.

His Honour gave a verdict for the defendant.

23/2/1868

WHY NOT SECURE YOUR BEDROOM DOOR? – A daring hotel robbery is reported from Nottingham. About seven o'clock on Wednesday morning, a man, described as of "gentlemanly exterior," sauntered into the bar of the Lion Hotel, Clumber-street, and, having ordered breakfast, obtained permission to go to the Commercial Room on an upper floor. On getting upstairs, it appears he tried several bedroom doors, and eventually got access to a room occupied by Mr North, a Sheffield hotel keeper. The gentleman was sleeping soundly, and, taking advantage of this circumstance, his visitor, it would seem, passed round his bed, rifled the pockets of his clothes of bank notes and cheques to the value of £50, £82 in gold, and a gold watch worth forty-two guineas, and stealing back through the bar unobserved, passed out of the hotel, and got away.

NOTICE TO BLACK PEOPLE ONLY. WANTED, TWO CHILDREN (Blacks or Mulattos), a Girl and a Boy, from Nine to Ten Years Old. Must be well made and smart, to be brought up in an English Family like their own children. For further particulars and information, address to Mrs BARTON, 30, Gloucester-street, Tower-street, Westminster-road, London.
N.B. – The English Family will leave London in the month of April, therefore an early application will oblige. This will be found an excellent opportunity for Children.
1/3/1868

THE SORROWS OF A POOR OLD ACTOR. – James Lee, an elderly man, who seemed quite broken down with care, was charged yesterday (Friday) before Mr Knox, at Marlborough-street Police-court, with begging in Burlington Arcade.

George Smith, the beadle of Burlington Arcade, said that on the previous evening some gentlemen in the Arcade complained of the prisoner asking them for charity, and on his hearing the prisoner ask a gentleman to assist him he took him into custody.

In answer to the charge, Lee said – I was not begging; I was only telling my misfortunes to the gentleman. I am a poor old used-up actor. I was born in 1798, and served my time at the Coburg Theatre, under the late Mr Glossop, and when the late Mr T.P. Cooke was the Stage-Manager. I have performed a great deal in the Provinces, and also in London Theatres. My wife, who is younger than myself, has been for four months in the London Hospital, under Drs Cooper and Adams, and has undergone several operations, and will most probably be lame for life. The last engagement I had was at the Agricultural Hall, with Messrs Sanger, and last winter I appeared as Pope Pius the Ninth, in *The Congress of Monarchs*. Since then Messrs Sanger have done a little for me, and are making a subscription amongst the company, with the view of assisting me in my distress. I have a prospect of getting a living shortly, though a very humble one, for my wife and myself. I was only stating my case, being a few weeks behind in my rent, when the officer came up.

Mr Knox – If I discharge you will you promise not to go to the place again. Lee – I will.

Mr Knox – Then you are discharged.

THE death is announced of a Welsh bard, Morgan Owen, at the age of eighty. It is stated that he had never been more than four miles away from home, had never written a letter during his life, neither had he ever received one.

Extraordinary Disturbance in a Theatre.
ON Saturday evening the Dunfermline Theatre* presented a scene the like of which was never before witnessed in the city. *Othello* was advertised to be performed – Miss Goddard to take the part of Othello, and Miss Clara Nash that of Desdemona. At seven o'clock, when the performance should have commenced, the Manager appeared on the stage in an excited state, and declared that he had lost £70, that he did not care for the audience, and that Miss Goddard would not play to such an audience. He went on making these statements for half an hour, and rating the audience in the gallery, who were very noisy, and they being impatient and displeased, he was loudly hooted and hissed at. After some time one of the actors appeared, and stated that Miss Goddard was ill, and not able to perform; but, with the permission of the audience, the company would go on with *The Dead Shot*, in which Miss Clara Nash took the principal part. This part of the performance went off pretty quietly.

The next performance was *Dick Turpin*, in which a horse and donkey appeared on the stage, but, not being trained, they did not give much satisfaction to the audience, who appeared determined to have *Othello* performed, and for a considerable time would not allow the performance to proceed. In consequence, it was gone through amid great uproar and confusion. The Manager was sadly abused and not one of the performers could, for more than an occasional interval, obtain a hearing. Several pieces of stick were thrown on the stage, and there were repeated cries for the Manager. While one of the actors was playing his part he was struck on the head by a marble, and, naturally enough, perhaps, losing his temper at this insult and injury, he exclaimed, "You are ------ contemptible hounds." One of the actresses urged him not to mind, but he continued, "What, not mind! I would not do so for the best man in the house; but if I could get hold of those who are throwing these marbles, I would bring this whip over their backs." This incident was the signal for the outbreak of another uproar. Another actor then appeared, and stated that Miss Goddard was dangerously ill, and that two doctors were attending her. These intimations were received with hissing, yelling, hooting, throwing of missiles of all descriptions, other marks of disapprobation.

Near the conclusion the Manager appeared and made some remarks, in the course of which he said "That he did not care a rap for the audience, and that they were a most unenlightened public." The Proprietor of the Theatre having been sent for, appeared and ordered the Manager to proceed, but it was some time before he left off expostulating and remonstrating with the audience. Ultimately he was compelled to leave the stage, and the play went on. The performers were not, however, heard, for the great noise which prevailed. They all, actresses as well as actors (Miss Nash excepted, who only appeared in the first play), endeavoured to obtain hearing to vindicate their own conduct. They were not allowed, however, for any length of time, but were received with marks of disapprobation. At the conclusion of the performance, the Proprietor expressed his regret at the misunderstanding which had taken place that night, and intimated that the season would close, and that before the Theatre was reopened extensive alterations would be made.

The theatre was the Corn Exchange, also known as the City Theatre.

A ROW ABOUT A POSTER. – The town of Newport in Monmouthshire was the scene of a misunderstanding a few days ago, and all about a placard of Mr Howard Paul as the Emperor Napoleon III, with which the town was freely posted by a committee of gentlemen who had projected an entertainment at the new Assembly Rooms. It seems the French Consul, in his fierce admiration of His Imperial Majesty, took exception to the aforesaid placard and complained to the Mayor, who in his turn had an interview with the superintendent of police, who, fired with a laudable desire to gratify the representative of France, caused all the portraits of His Majesty to be covered. This of course exasperated the amusement committee, who were up in arms against this irregular proceeding, and the consequence was not only an *emeute* between the authorities and those interested in the exhibition of the pictures, but the walls were covered with squibs against the zeal of the Mayor and the officious sensibility of the French Consul. It turns out that these very portraits of Napoleon III were executed in France, and are in constant sale in the streets of Paris as admirable portraits of the French Emperor, an announcement which greatly extinguished the ardour of the Newport Consul.

FRIGHTFUL ACCIDENT TO A "TRAPEZE" PERFORMER. – The *Dundee Advertiser* reports a lamentable accident which befell a gymnast – one of the Brothers Bellena – at the Dundee Music Hall on the 27th ult. The brothers went through some very clever and daring gymnastic performances, which many of the audience, especially females, could not behold except with fear, but for which they received from the greater bulk of those present the warmest approbation. The older and stronger of the two hung from the trapeze by the legs, while he caught the younger by one of the hands as he was falling past him, and swung him in the air. This and other equally daring feats, as we have already stated, were accomplished in safety.

The next exhibition of their agility was intended to be of a similar kind. The elder of the two swung from the trapeze by the legs, and while in this state it was evidently his intention to catch the younger by the left ankle. By some miscalculation, however, the leg of the younger brother came some few inches

short of the reach of the other, and he fell head foremost into the orchestra. The sensation created amongst the audience on witnessing such a spectacle can better be imagined than described. Screams and sobs escaped from men and women, and a number of those in the front seats rushed in a state of excitement to see whether the unfortunate performer had been killed by his fearful fall. The poor fellow, when picked up from amongst the feet of the band, lay in the arms of his supporters in a state of unconsciousness, with the blood flowing from a wound in the skull. He alighted with his head on the sharp edge of the footstool used by the leader of the orchestra with such force that he broke it, after having struck in his descent the neck of a violin. On examination, it was found that he had sustained a large scalp wound of semicircular shape, and about three or four inches in length, on the crown of the head, and some slight bruises on the forehead, but, so far as could be seen, he did not appear to have sustained any very serious injury. Falling a distance of upwards of twenty feet, and alighting on the crown of his head, it is a wonder that he was not killed on the spot. It is supposed that he must have saved himself by his hands from receiving the full force of the fall.
8/3/1868

MADAME RACHEL'S QUEENLY LILY WATER of CIRCASSIA, CIRCASSIAN and ARABIAN GEMS of the TOILET, and ARABIAN LIQUID ENAMEL, impart a rich Golden Hue to the Hair, give Sparkling Brilliancy to the Eyes, a Soft, Youthful, and Radiant Beauty to the Face, Neck, and Arms, Pearly Whiteness to the Teeth, Ruby Lips, and impart a Soft Odour to the Skin. These Costly and Fashionable Preparations give Youth and Beauty to persons Freckled, Scarred, or Aged – all that can enhance and preserve the charms of woman, and which have gained for her a world-renowned name as the Great Beautifier to the Royal Courts of Europe. All other persons vending dangerous and destructive compounds in imitation commit a gross fraud upon the public. 47A, New Bond-street; and 30, Rue de la Paix, and 15, Rue de Choiseul, Paris.
22/3/1868

COUNTING SHRIMPS. – A singular case of cumulative penalties occurred at Macclesfield a few days ago. A fishmonger was summoned for having on sale a quantity of shrimps in a decomposed state and unfit for human food. The police inspector said he had counted the shrimps, that there were 2040, and that defendant being liable to pay a fine of £20 for each shrimp, the total amount of the penalties would be £40,800. The Magistrates were doubtless delighted that the arithmetical shrewdness of the inspector gave them such an excellent opportunity for proving the "unstrained quality of mercy," and they, therefore, remitted £40,799 of the penalty, and fined the lucky fishmonger 20s. only.

A NEW SENSATION. – AUSTRALIAN ABORIGINAL CRICKETERS, Native Black Australians, and the first Australian Aborigines who have visited England, will arrive in the Country early in May, to compete in Cricket Matches and give illustrations of Australian National Sports, combined with European. Amongst these will be Spear and Boomerang Throwing, the Corroboree, Jumping, and Running. They were Trained in Australia by Mr W.R. Hayman, of Devonshire, and will be Captained by Mr Charles Lawrence, formerly of the All-England Eleven. Applications for Provincial Matches and Sports to be addressed to Mr E.P. HINGSTON, Spiers and Pond's, 38, New Bridge-street, E.C., London.
29/3/1868

SWIMMING ON THE STAGE. – VICTORIA THEATRE. – Professor BECKWITH and his Amphibious Family in a Monstre Plate Glass Aquarium, on THURSDAY night next, for their BENEFIT, when they have been promised the assistance of some of the Celebrities of the Musical and Sporting World, besides the Talented Company Engaged at this Theatre. For other particulars, see Monstre Bills. Open at Hippodrome, Paris, shortly. Great Success at Liverpool, Manchester, and Birmingham. Address, BECKWITH, Lambeth Baths, London.
5/4/1868

"Penny Readings" and Amateur Actors.
TO THE EDITOR OF THE ERA.
Sir, – May I so far presume upon your kindness as to crave the insertion of this letter in the columns of your admirably-conducted paper? There is a general complaint among that great number of Professionals, whose business lies in the Provinces, in reference to the extremely bad nature of the business they are at present doing. By some this depression is attributed to the fact of its having been Lent, &c., and by others to the bad state of trade generally. But making all due allowance for both the above causes, there is one great and particular reason why Professionals find it so hard to get a living just now. It is simply owing to the fact that the clergymen in almost all small towns (at least all that I have visited in the last six months), while they revile, libel, and do their best to injure the private character of all Professionals, from their pulpits every Sunday, during the week superintend the getting-up, and patronise the performances, by what is termed "local talent!"

Now I admire talent – *real talent unalloyed by impudence* – as much as anyone possibly can, but I certainly think that the task of amusing the public ought to be left in the hands of those whose business it legitimately is. It is in vain that drapers' clerks and grocers' assistants seek to combine the trade with the Profession. A class of *home made* Professionals never have been, never are, and never will be, amusing. It is as difficult to learn to walk on and off the stage properly as it is to acquire the art of being a clergyman. In fact, I think more so, for I have seen many a noted and popular preacher who would have made a sorry mess of Rosencranz or Seyton.

Now, as long as they confine themselves to an occasional Penny Reading I don't much care, although the name itself is a falsehood, as the Penny admission is now almost entirely obsolete, and they charge two shillings, a shilling, and sixpence, with all possible assurance; but what I do object to is, their attempting to completely shut up, starve out, and utterly destroy the Profession at large; while they sanctimoniously "pocket the coppers," and all the time do exactly what they condemn us for doing. They are not content, now, with penny readings – that is neither with the *penny* nor the *readings*. They play pieces, regular three act dramas, with a full cast. Not long since I came across a tribe of pious amateurs playing *The Lady of Lyons*, and when I reminded them of the fact that by doing so they were infringing the laws of the Dramatic Authors' Society, the "Claude" of the evening coolly observed that it was all right, as IT WAS UNDER THE VICAR'S PATRONAGE. (I need not tell you what the performance was like.)

Not in one or two but in a dozen consecutive towns has this been the case, and so strongly is the feeling "worked up" that in many towns we have been almost unable to get lodgings, the people evidently suspecting that we are not so respectable as we should be. It is with Professionals themselves whether they are respected or despised, and did they ALL behave with thorough propriety, there is no reason why they should not be as highly respected as the clergy themselves, for a public entertainer is a public benefactor.

I would respectfully ask, are there no means by which the right of entertaining the public may be ceded to those who have spent time, money, and study in learning to do it properly? The clergyman in his right place is to the majority an object of respect, but when he descends from the pulpit, and seeks to make a *soi-disant* showman of himself, he becomes simply an object of ridicule.

Apologising for the space I have occupied, I have the honour to be yours respectfully, FRED. MEDEX, Bungay, Suffolk, April 18th.

NATATOR, the Human Frog, is now fulfilling a most Successful Engagement at the CIRQUE NAPOLEON, PARIS, in his New and Elegant Aquarium, accompanied with large Carp and Tench, which appear to treat him as one of themselves. Terms and dates, Mr CHARLES SPENCER, 35, Old-street, London, E.C.
19/4/1868

Extraordinary Suicide of one of the Brothers Hanlon.

THE well known gymnast, Mr Thomas Hanlon, eldest of the popular and widely known Hanlon Brothers, met with his death in Harrisburg, PA., on Sunday morning, the 5th inst., at half-past three o'clock. He performed at the Metropolitan Theatre, Indianapolis, Ind., on Monday evening, March 30th, with his combination, in apparently as good health as ever, and nothing wrong was noticeable by anyone. At breakfast, the next morning, he ate very little, after which he commenced smoking a cigar, and stated to his brothers that he was going to New York.

Nothing more was heard of him by his relatives until Friday morning, when they received a telegram from the Mayor of Harrisburg stating that he, with his three pupils, was in that city and under arrest. It appears that Mr Thomas Hanlon arrived at the State Capitol Hotel, Harrisburg, on Thursday morning, the 2nd inst., with his three pupils, and he first attracted the attention of the landlord by acting in a strange manner. He said that he had been down town and everyone had laughed at him. He then disappeared, and at noon the three boys were found at the depot crying and hunting for Thomas, who was found in the vicinity of the market house, and not being known was locked up in the station-house overnight. The following morning it was discovered who he was, and he was taken to the hotel, where he took breakfast, soon after which he was found walking along the river bank; and the remarks he made and his strange manner led parties to believe that he was going to commit suicide. He was arrested, but not without a fierce struggle.

Shortly after his confinement in his cell he was given some dinner on a tin plate, and, breaking the plate in two, tried to cut his throat with it. Seeing a bar over his cell door he was about to hang himself from it when he was removed to another cell. Under the floor of this cell was an iron steam pipe which heats the cells in winter. Where the pipes join each other at the extreme end of the cell was a small brass nut, projecting from the floor about three inches. Hearing a great noise the officers entered the apartment and found him in his shirt sleeves. From twelve to fifteen times did he start from the door of the cell, spring into the air, and, gathering himself, turned a half somersault each time and and came down full force, driving his head down upon this sharp nut. This he continued to do until six men entered the cell to bind him; but he seemed to be endowed with superhuman power, for he threw them off as if they were children, and drove them from the place, cutting one over the eye and breaking the nose of another. The officers no sooner left than he renewed the attempt to kill himself, and he presented a horrible sight. The whole of his scalp was cut away and hanging in strips down over his face, while the blood was streaming all over his person and the floor of the cell. He finally became exhausted from the great loss of blood, and, instead of continuing his leaping into the air, laid down and tried to dash out his brains by beating his head against the brass cock.

Another rush was made by the officers, and this time they overpowered him and brought him into the corridor, where he dashed his head against the brick floor with tremendous force. Chloroform was then administered to him and his arms were pinioned behind him, and he was tied down to a bed with a sheet. A doctor brought the pieces of cut and mangled scalp together and secured them by sutures. After sleeping off the potion he awoke and appeared in a rational frame of mind, asked for some toast and boiled eggs, which were given him, but it would not stay on his stomach. He shortly after became delirious and remained so up to the last, when he died as stated above. Mr George W. Roney (formerly with the other branch of the Hanlons), Edward Hanlon and Harry Gurr reached the bedside of Thomas about fifteen minutes before he died.

The body arrived in New York on Monday morning, about half-past five, in charge of his brother Edward, and was taken to the undertaker's. […]

A LADY CHARGED WITH HAVING FOUR HUSBANDS.

AT the Southwark Police-court last Tuesday a tall, handsome, and fashionably dressed lady, who was described on the charge sheet as Mrs Rickaby, twenty-four years of age, of independent means, was brought before Mr Burcham charged with intermarrying with Robert Mills, Charles Reeves, and Humphrey Purcell Blackmore, her first husband being then and now living. The prisoner was attired in travelling costume, and had with her two valuable dogs, a pair of canaries, and a large quantity of luggage.

Mr H.W. Vallance, who appeared for the prosecution, said that he was instructed by Dr Blackmore, a physician, residing at Salisbury, who had married the prisoner at Perth on 1st of October last, to proceed against the prisoner for bigamy, and on the previous day they traced her from Exeter to London, coming up in the same train, and on their arrival they had a constable in attendance at the Waterloo Terminus, to whom he gave her into custody. He was not prepared to go into all the facts of the case that day, but he would give sufficient evidence to warrant a remand.

Mr Vallance was then sworn, and produced copies of certificates of the marriage of the prisoner with Charles Reeves, of Cardiff, on the 2nd of June, 1863, and on the 22nd of January, 1866, at Carlisle, with Robert Mills, and lastly with his client, Mr Humphrey Purcell Blackmore, physician, Salisbury, on 1st October last at Perth. During all the marriages her first husband was living.

Mr Vallance said it was a painful thing for him to prosecute the prisoner, whose connections were highly respectable, but he had a duty to perform to his client and to the public. He therefore asked for a remand to enable him to produce evidence of the former marriages.

Mr Burcham accordingly remanded her until Monday next, agreeing to accept two sureties in £100 each for her appearance.

Bail not being forthcoming she was remanded to Horsemonger-lane Gaol.

She was later sentenced to one months' imprisonment.

THE BALLET GIRL'S HARDSHIPS. – A NEEDLESS FATE. – Have our readers ever reflected on the courage required in the ballet dancer's profession? The risks she runs are hardly less frequent and far more formidable than those which the soldier of the line or the man-of-war's-man gets so much credit for facing. It is one thing to take your chance of being sabred or hit by a bullet; but is is another and (to our mind) a much more terrible ordeal to pirouette in combustible gauze before the foot-lights, or, worse still, be pinioned to an iron niche in some brilliant transformation scene, and to remain immoveably fixed to your precarious perch, amid a blaze of light and within the leap of the flames from a thousand burners. Yet this is the experience which myriads of poor girls have to encounter night after night, that juveniles might be entertained and gaudy crowds amused.

A girl of this ill-starred profession, whose skirts caught fire at a Concert Hall in Birmingham on the evening of Friday, the 20th ult., died on the morning of Monday following – adding another to the hecatomb of such victims yearly sacrificed to a frivolous and callous public. Is Parliament never to legislate against the use of inflammable raiment? Is humanity always to be murmuring, *quosque tandem**? Till the state interfere, and compel Managers of Theatres and Proprietors of Music Halls to protect their employees of the ballet by the precautions which chemistry furnishes against fire, we shall continue to be horrified by such instances as that just announced from Birmingham, and to regard our places of scientific amusement as fraught with deaths of greater torture than those of the bull of Phalaris**. – The Lancet*

*For how much longer?
**An instrument of torture supposedly used by Phalaris, the tyrant of Sicily; it took the form of a hollow brass bull in which prisoners were roasted alive.*
26/4/1868

CRYSTAL PALACE. – WILD ROSE, the Blue and Flesh-coloured Hairless Mare, exhibited in the Tropical Department, is one of the most extraordinary Exhibitions ever offered. This beautiful creature, now perfectly docile, was found in Africa, in the midst of a Herd of Quaggas. It has been visited already by thousands of visitors, who are delighted with it. Whit-Monday, Twentieth Week.

DEATH OF A CANINE CELEBRITY. – Messrs Phillips and Preston's clever performing Newfoundland dog, Hector, died at Aldershot on Wednesday, May 27th. During the last twelve years he has appeared at all the principal Theatres and Music Halls in Great Britain with unparalled success, and was a great favourite both with the Profession and public. He was stuffed by Mr E. Lees, the eminent naturalist of the Military Train, Aldershot, and buried by the side of J. Emmett's performing dog, Dick. He was over fifteen years of age, and his last appearance on the stage was at the Theatre Royal, Leicester, May 18th, in the drama of *The Woodman and his Dogs*.

A GENTLEMAN, educated at a Public School, wishes to read SHAKESPEARE and other Poets in Public, and only wants a Capitalist to Join him. The Advertiser will call at any hour on any Gentleman answering this in *The Era*, and give references both as to his position, and also of his Reading Capabilities.
31/5/1868

MISS HERBERT. – The lady now holding Dramatic Classes, and who has been playing in the above name at Sadler's Wells Theatre, is not in any way related or connected with Miss Herbert of the St. James's Theatre. Her real and professional name is Rosina Pennell. She is the niece of Admiral Waldren Pennell and Lady Barrow, and has been in the Profession eleven years.
7/6/1868

A BALLOON BURNT. – A newly-constructed aerial machine, by Mr Hodsman, of Dublin, was totally destroyed at the Chester Railway Station, owing to spontaneous combustion, just as it was proceeding to Bradford for ascents during the Whitsuntide holidays. The misfortune led to an immediate application to Mr Coxwell, who possesses a perfect fleet of balloons, and that celebrated gentleman himself proceeded by return train to Yorkshire, and was just in time to make two fine ascents, and prevent public disappointment at Peel Park, Bradford.

TO THE EDITOR OF THE ERA.
Sir, – In *The Era* of the 7th inst. I noticed a paragraph respecting a Miss Herbert, late of Sadler's Wells Theatre, but "now holding dramatic classes," on which I presume to make one or two comments. I am the son of the Admiral alluded to, and, consequently, the nephew of her Ladyship, his sister, but I never, until this moment, knew that I had a cousin in any way connected with the Theatrical Profession.

It is not my intention to question the veracity of the statement, nor is it worth my while to request an explanation of the same, but I must say that, by whomsoever written, no small amount of bad taste was shown in thus wantonly dragging the names of two of the lady's titled relatives (if they are, indeed, such) into print, and in support of so frivolous and immaterial a point. I do not insinuate for a moment that the fact of the lady being on the stage is in any way derogatory to herself or family, but I think, out of mere delicacy, the names of those whose principles prevent them from regarding the Drama in its brightest light might have been omitted. I am, Sir, your obedient servant, C.M.C.P.
14/6/1868

MISS LYDIA HOWARD, THE BABY ACTRESS.
SINCE the 3rd inst., this extraordinarily gifted child has been giving her entertainments at the Westbourne Hall, Westbourne-grove, Bayswater. Little Lydia is now only in her fifth year, and shows an aptitude for acting which must strike all who see her as something marvellous. Her self-possession and earnestness in the work before her is far beyond anything that could be expected from a child of such tender years, and the entire performance is, perhaps, a more astounding instance of juvenile precocity than has ever been brought before the English public. The child's powers of memory alone are astonishing. Prompters

are, of course, at hand, but she never falters or hesitates, and acts, and sings, and dances with a sprightliness and vivacity that, so far as we are aware, is absolutely unparalleled in the juvenile world.

The night we attended a burlesque on the nursery story *Little Red Riding Hood* stood first on the programme. In this the "Baby Actress" sustained the characters of Red Riding Hood and the Fairy, whose sudden appearance leads the "naughty Duke" to repent of his evil deeds, and to alter the course of his life. The child sang the song "A Frog he would a-wooing go," and joined with Mr Howard (her father) in a duet. The latter played the Grandmother and the Naughty Duke in league with the Ogre partial to dining upon the flesh of young girls. The Leading Lady is incomparably the best of Miss Howard's performances, and her assumption of consequential dignity is the most amusing thing conceivable. Mr Howard performs the Manager hectored and imposed upon by this peremptory little lady, who refuses to speak a word until her salary is raised, and a brougham is placed at her disposal. In a scene from the old burlesque, *Bombastes Furioso*, the diminutive Lydia personates Distaffina, and sings the refrain of a Music Hall song called "The bell goes a-ringing for Sarah." She also gives a verse of "Barney O'Hea," and part of another song. In masculine full dress she sings W. Lingard's song "The Upper Ten," and shows a most acute perception of character. [...]
21/6/1868

TO THE EDITOR OF THE ERA.
Sir, – In answer to a letter from "C.M.C.P." which appeared in your columns of the 14th inst., I beg to say I was requested by my husband to change my own and original name, which I first played in (in 1857), to that of Herbert, as I still wished to follow my Profession and organised dramatic classes, and as I did not then (nor do I now) wish to cause any annoyance to my father's family by having a name that stands so *high* for ever in public print, I was willing to do so. However, that does not alter the fact that the Admiral and her Ladyship were my late father's brother and sister. Apologising for trespassing so much on your valuable space, I am, Sir, yours obediently, R.H.P.
28/6/1868

THEATRICAL LITIGATION.
WESTMINSTER COUNTY COURT, JULY 6th (Before J. BAYLEY, ESQ., Judge).
AN EXTRAORDINARY CASE. – In the present action Mr Montague appeared for the plaintiff; and Mr Baker Green, instructed by Edward Lewis and Co., of Great Marlborough-street, was retained for the defendant. The plaintiff was formerly an actress in the service of the defendant, who was Manager of the French *troupe* lately occupying the boards of the St James's Theatre, whom she sued for £40 for one month's salary and wrongful dismissal. She stated in evidence that she had travelled in many parts of the Continent with the defendant, but at his request consented to accompany the French *troupe* to England. As both plaintiff and defendant were unable to speak English, their evidence was interpreted by M. Albert.

Mdlle Hudemarde, sworn, stated that she was engaged in June of last year by the defendant, and put in the agreement entered into with the defendant, and was re-engaged in October of the same year. I arrived in London on the 9th of that month, and was perfectly able to take any part assigned to me until 31st May.

Cross-examined by Mr Baker Green – I was *enceinte* when in Paris, but the defendant made no objection. Before coming to London the defendant stated he should not require my services, but when at Bucharest he offered to pay my expenses to London that I should be confined there rather than among my friends in Paris. The pregnancy of a married lady under similar circumstances does not vitiate an engagement. It is merely considered as an illness, and she continues to act so long as she is able. The defendant detained my salary in case he should suffer any loss by my confinement. I was able to play during the whole of May and two weeks afterwards. It was not my wish that my name should be struck out of the bills.

Madame Hudemarde – I am the mother of the plaintiff, and was with my daughter during the whole of her engagement with the defendant, and she was perfectly able to sustain all the parts assigned to her.

Dr Bernardet, a French physician, residing in Manchester-street, Manchester-square – I was consulted by the plaintiff, who I found to be six months in the family way. At the termination of engagement she was physically able to walk the stage and play her parts. Her pregnancy was hardly perceptible, and she could easily play boys' parts without her condition being discovered.

Mr Raphael Felix, the defendant, stated that before arriving at Bucharest I made some observations to the plaintiff on the subject of her pregnancy, and wished her to rescind the contract, which, if she did not do, I would enforce it. She came over to this country with Mr Ravel's troupe to the St James's Theatre, and I only saw her when she came to be paid, and even before leaving Bucharest I was obliged, owing to her state, to engage another lady in her place, as her appearance would not have been creditable in London. I swear that in France I have known several contracts rescinded under similar circumstances.

After some discussion between the counsel on both sides, his Honour postponed the case till the 15th inst., when further evidence would be adduced as to the validity of the contract.

Beheading a Lady.
TO THE EDITOR OF THE ERA.
Sir, – This trick was exhibited at the Princess's Theatre, Leeds, in December, 1863, in the following manner: Miss Marguerite Thorne recited a portion of the poem called "Pharanthe." A man dressed as an Egyptian advanced, and led her towards the back of the stage, where (to the accompaniment of solemn music) she knelt at a block, the executioner appeared to give a tremendous blow with an axe, and her head fell to the ground. The trunk then stood erect; its hand was led gently to the head, which it grasped by its long hair. The trunk then, apparently, held its head at arm's length, and the head spoke the remainder of the poem. The lady's voice and features were so well known that no mask could have been used, and the entertainment (!) would have been repeated the following week but that the *Leeds Express* characterised it as "too appalling." The exhibitor was Mr C. Rice, author of *The Stricken Oak*, then playing. Yours truly, THE LIME-LIGHTER.

The Jolliest Dogs that are out are SAMWELL'S DOGS – Dogmatically Speaking, are *Dog Stars*, especially the *Spotted Dog*, A 1 K 9 Clown, whose antics keep the audience in a roar of laughter. This Wonderful Dog was reared by a *Comical Puppy*, fed on the *bark of witty instinct* and w(h)ine of *humour*, and taught by *Le Chien des Chiens droles* in a *Foreign Kennel*. Now to be seen Performing every Evening at the AMPHITHEATRE CIRCUS, HOLBORN.
We've Clowns who are great,
And Clowns who are small;
We've Clowns in the world,
Who're no Clowns at all;
We've Clowns make you smile,
As onward you jog;
But the greatest of Clowns
Is Samwell's Dog!
Each night at the Amphi –
Believe it, no chaff –
That Dog keeps the audience
In one continual laugh! – *Vide*, the London Press.
12/7/1868

FEARFUL FALL OF AN ACROBAT. – A man of colour, styling himself "The Great African Blondin," has been amusing the people at Beverley this week by walking upon a rope at an altitude of fifty feet.

On Wednesday night, the performer made his appearance as usual, and, having addressed the people below, he commenced his perilous journey amidst much cheering. He had only traversed half the length of the narrow road, however, before the rope gave a sudden "snap," and the hapless performer the next instant (with the balancing pole in his hands) was seen falling from his giddy height to the ground. The performer lay upon the ground, face downwards, with the balancing pole under him, apparently lifeless; but on the arrival of medical men it was found that he still lived. A cab was procured, in which he was conveyed to his lodgings, in Walkergate, and on further examination it was found that he had broken one of his arms and wrists. He lies in a very precarious state.
19/7/1868

THE FATAL PANIC AT A MANCHESTER MUSIC HALL.
OUR readers are by this time acquainted with the principal features of the late disastrous panic at the Victoria Music Hall, Manchester, which occurred at about ten o'clock on the evening of Friday, the 31st ult., and consequently at too late an hour to be reported in our impression of last Saturday. […] The original proprietor was Mr Benjamin Lang, and in consequence the Music Hall came to be known amongst its patrons as "Ben Lang's," a name which it still retains, although Mr Lang has long since retired from all connection with it. "Ben Lang's" enjoyed an extensive popularity amongst the working class population of Manchester and Salford, and even of the manufacturing districts around Manchester, whose inhabitants generally paid "Ben's" a visit when business or pleasure took them to Manchester.

We are not sure that the class of visitors has not of late years begun to deteriorate; certain it is that the low charges of admission – threepence to the pit, and twopence to the gallery – have had the effect of introducing a juvenile element into the audience, which could scarcely be expected to improve the tone of the place. It must not be supposed, however, that there was anything seriously objectionable either in the character of the entertainment, which was occasionally vulgar, as, we regret to say, this class of entertainment sometimes is, or in the moral constitution of the audience, which, though somewhat unruly in behaviour, had less of absolute vice in its ranks than was to be found at more pretentious places of amusement.

The ground floor of the building is occupied by a vault, shop, and offices of various kinds – all, however, included in the establishment of which the Music Hall was the principal feature. The latter comprised the first, second, and third floors of the building, which formed the pit, lower, and upper galleries, the floors in each part of the house being perfectly level, and the seats receiving the requisite incline by a rude contrivance which added to the elevation of the flooring. The lighting and ventilation of the place were of a primitive description, and to illuminate the pit pendant chandeliers, the burners unprotected by glass, hung from underneath the galleries. The approaches to the auditorium, particularly the galleries, were not of the best description, for although the passages were of moderate width, averaging about a yard and a half, the stairs were so steep and took so many bends, and the edges of the steps being, moreover, protected by clamps of iron, that neither comfort nor entire safety could be said to be secured to the visitors when their numbers, as on the fatal Friday night, were large. An iron rail, running down the centre of the staircase, formed, it should be observed, a very useful and necessary support to cling by, though its object was probably to separate persons going in from those returning.

On the evening in question Mr and Mrs H. Clifford, comic duettists, were to take their benefit, and as an additional inducement prizes were offered for the best and "worst" amateur comic singer, each competitor to hold a live goose under his arm during his musical effort. (This condition, we understand, was actually complied with.) Another attraction was a sack race across the stage. It was just as the latter item of the programme was in progress that the incident occurred which wrought all this mischief.

It is said that several boys, eager to witness the performance, stood up and endeavoured to steady themselves by clutching the frail gas-pipe hanging from the gallery above them; others, that a man in the pit endeavoured to light his pipe at the chandelier, and that it broke while he held on to it; at all events, the pipe did break and the gas escaped. One of the officials of the establishment promptly plugged the pipe, and the people in the pit, where the circumstance happened, were not in the least troubled; but the smell of the escaped gas had reached the gallery, and a cry of "Fire!" raised by someone in the lower gallery, was sufficient to strike terror into those who occupied the galleries. Instantly a mad rush took place for the staircase.

In vain Mr Clifford and others shouted that there was no danger, and begged them to remain quiet. Those in the pit were orderly, and obeyed the injunctions; but the panic had got the better of the reason of the rest, and they rushed pell-mell down the steps till some of them losing their footing at an awkward turn of the stairs others were precipitated over them, till at length the passage was blocked, and a vast number of persons were thrown together in one hideous jumble, from which they were only extricated by the police and officials of the Hall on the other side, who dragged the bodies out by main force. And out of that ghastly heap were picked twenty-three dead bodies, chiefly of young people, from twelve to twenty, suffocated in that frantic crush, their bodies bruised and trodden under foot, and the clothing in some cases torn from their backs, everything thus showing the terrible nature of the struggle. The dead and injured were removed with all possible speed to the infirmary, where all attention was paid to those requiring assistance. By the latest accounts TWENTY-THREE persons were found to have been KILLED and twelve injured; all the latter, with one exception, being in a fair way of recovery. The exception referred to is a boy suffering from concussion of the brain.

The Hall itself sustained no material damage; a number of the benches were broken. The iron rail which divided the gallery staircase had given way under the pressure at the point where the block took place, and even one of the steps, fortified as it was by the iron plating we have mentioned, was completely smashed. These with the exception of a few broken windows were all the damages the Hall received.

Mr Davies, the Proprietor, was absent in Buxton when the panic occurred. On his return, which was of course immediate, he issued bills and advertisements offering £20 reward for the person who raised the cry of fire. The Hall was open on Monday night as usual to the public, and the ordinary entertainments proceeded.

9/8/1868

WONDERS NEVER CEASE. To Music Halls, Theatres, Gardens, and Circuses. – Something New. THE MULATTO LADY, a native of Calcutta, the Champion Female Walker of the World, who caused such a great sensation in Yorkshire (four years ago) *Fete*, walking One Mile round the stage in eleven minutes, and sings her great 1,000 Miles Walking Song, and another. She appears in her native costume. For dates, address J. ATKINSON, Wellington-place, Wellington-lane, West-street, Leeds.

Improvisation, Vocalisation, Instrumentation. – Unprecedented and Brilliant Success. CHARLES SLOMAN, the only English Improvisatore, at HUNGERFORD MUSIC HALL, VILLIERS-STREET, STRAND, every Evening, at Half-past Nine. A Challenge – Come one, come all. Propound your subjects. No matter whether Classic, Historic, or Scientific, so that they be not political, personal, or theological, and he will deliver Poems upon them in extemporaneous verse, a display of mental power unattempted by any other literary exhibitant. At Liberty for one Turn, at Nine or Eleven. Private address, 10, Bury-street, Bloomsbury, W.C.

16/8/1868

NOVELTY. – Managers can have the greatest Wonder out, THE BROTHERS BOW WOW, Gymnastic and Acrobatic Canine Wonders (Four in Number) – Diamond, Pearl, Tim, and Fleet. Diamond leaps seven feet high and twenty in length. Pearl holds hoops for his brother's leaps. For dates and terms apply to DOHERTY, Clown, Vauxhall Gardens, Ipswich.

EXTRAORDINARY UPROAR at ST JAMES'S THEATRE.

LAST night an "extraordinary performance," in every sense of the phrase, took place at this Theatre. The "Great Mexican Tragedian" was announced to play in *Richard the Third*, and there was a good audience, considering the season, assembled in the house. The play commenced, but the performance did not work smoothly – to put the matter in the most harmonious manner possible – and at the close of the second act an attempted apology was made from the stage to the effect that the Management had no funds. The uproar that followed may be better imagined than described. The "gods" at once proceeded to show that they had the spirit of their fathers in them by tearing up the seats, but a few of the "victims" behind the scenes acted as constables, thus preventing an uproar from terminating in a calamity. The Theatre was altogether closed before ten o'clock.

23/8/1868

A THEATRICAL SCANDAL.

"A DO, A DO, A PALPABLE DO."

We have had many times to complain of Theatrical "Jeremy Diddlers*," who are in the habit of taking Theatres in the Provinces with no other capital than sheer impudence, and who, therefore, too often leave the poor actors in the lurch, *sans* money, *sans* credit, *sans* everything; but anything more barefaced or more disgraceful than the recent proceedings at the St James's Theatre never came under our notice, and we trust that some means will be found of introducing the parties concerned to one of the Metropolitan Magistrates, if not to a higher tribunal. Our readers will recollect with what a flourish of trumpets "Don Edgardo di Colona," the Great Mexican Tragedian, the "only successor to Kean and Macready," who brought with him testimonials of his genius from President Juarez, and other competent authorities, was lately announced to appear at the St James's Theatre; but few could have suspected that the Mr Walter St John, under whose auspices he was to appear, and who called himself the Manager of the Theatre, was literally a penniless adventurer, and that the company got together so regardless of expense that it was necessary to announce that there would be "no increase in prices" were destined never to receive one farthing for their services; nay, more, that a large number, if not the majority, of its members had been actually cajoled into paying for their engagements; yet such were the facts.

It appears that, on the 19th of June, an advertisement appeared in the papers stating that any lady or gentleman aspirant for the stage might "obtain a fine opening at a first-class London Theatre" by applying, &c., &c. The bait took, and applicants were, in due time, answered by a so-called theatrical agent, bearing a foreign patronymic, offering an engagement at the St James's Theatre for a month, for which the applicants were called upon to pay £10, or rather to take £10 worth of tickets. The amount appears to have been pretty generally objected to, but we are assured that, in several cases, the full £10 was paid, whilst in others it was generously reduced, the rule apparently being to take whatever could be got. In one case a gentleman, whose name and address we have, paid £10, and received a written agreement for a month, at a salary of £1 10s. per week, and in another a lady, who, though an English woman, has spent the greater part of her life on the Continent, studying for the stage, paid £4 in cash, and received an agreement that she should have £2 a week, and be brought out as Lady Macbeth between the 15th and 29th of August, and in the meantime be placed in such other characters as were "not derogatory" to a leading lady, it being provided that, in addition to the £4 paid, her first week's salary was to go to the agent, or, in other words, she was to pay £6 for a fortnight's engagement at £2 per week. By these means, it would appear that a sufficient sum was got together to open the Theatre, and accordingly, on the 15th, the great Don Edgardo di Colona made his appearance as Richard the Third. Of the nature of the performance we need say nothing now, as we have already expressed our opinion, which has been unanimously endorsed by our daily contemporaries; but to the result, and this we will give in the words of the Stage-Manager, who writes to explain that he was in no way connected with the proceedings beyond having accepted a professional engagement. He says: –

"A full company, band, and thoroughly efficient staff, were engaged. The Theatre opened, business continuing pretty fair through the week, but when the hour announced for treasury came on Saturday morning, a notice was put up to the effect that 'treasury' would be postponed until night. From this moment the imposture revealed itself; the company and employees became uneasy. Night came, verifying the suspicions aroused by the postponement of the morning. After paying a few miserable installments, with lame excuse and promise, to one or two of the people, the carpenters and band struck in the course of the performance for the residue of their money, bringing the 'speculator' to a standstill. He then, for the first time, openly and coolly announced that he had "no money." Upon being questioned by myself and other members of the company as to what had become of the receipts, he could neither make any satisfactory reply, nor render any acceptable account of the moneys taken (presumed about £120)."

Of course all the parties engaged did not pay, some respectable members of the Profession having been enlisted to add grace to the bill by their names, and to apparently act as decoy ducks to others; but all were treated alike with regard to salary. We do not at present mention the name of the agent, because he will, we trust, come forward and explain his share in the transaction, and return the moneys received for obtaining the engagements; if he does not, we are persuaded that an application to a Magistrate or a County Court action would compel him to do so; if, indeed, it has not been shared with others, and dissipated beyond redemption.

We shall say nothing about these after seasons, as they are called, at the London Theatres, as we are aware that in many instances they have been the means of introducing to the public, and, we may say, to the Profession itself, ladies and gentlemen who but for the opportunities so afforded them of showing what they could do, might have struggled many years without obtaining that position due to their talent. In these cases, however, pecuniary rewards are not generally looked for in the first instance; and no person is justified in taking a Theatre, even for the purpose of testing his own success with the public, unless he has the means of paying those whom he engages to assist him.

We cannot, however, altogether hold actors blameless who accept engagements from unknown adventurers without some assurance that, at least, their first week's salary is secured beyond the power of the Managers to convert it to their own use, whilst the Proprietors of Theatres only bring discredit on their houses when they let them to such persons. We are aware that they generally secure themselves by having their rent in advance, but that is not enough; they are bound, for the credit of their Theatre, if not for the honour of their Profession, to see that it does not pass, even for a time, into discreditable hands; and we feel assured that no one will more deeply regret the recent proceedings at the St James's Theatre than Miss Herbert, the justly popular Lessee of the establishment.

Jeremy Diddler: a con-man in James Kenney's 1803 farce Raising the Wind.

ATTEMPTED ROBBERY FROM AN ACTOR. – As Mr Charles E. Walsh, who is attached to the company at the Prince of Wales Theatre, Birmingham, was returning home after the performance on Saturday, the 22nd inst., he was met near the Tindal-bridge, King Edward's-road, by a man who demanded a shilling from him. Mr Walsh refused to accede to his request, and the man made a snatch and seized his watch chain, Mr Walsh managing to hold fast to his watch. The man then struck him a violent blow on the eye, which felled him to the ground. He still, however, retained his hold upon the watch, and the man at length ran off, pursued by Mr Walsh to the side of the canal, where, through exhaustion, he was compelled to give up the pursuit. The blow was a very severe one, the flesh being cut to the bone. However, Mr Walsh is expected to resume his character of Pandulph in *King John* this (Saturday) evening.
30/8/1868

DEATH FROM AN ARROW. – A little girl, named Clara Louisa Bingham, while lying on the grass during the Foresters' Fete in Vintners Park, near Maidstone, was struck by a stray arrow, shot from the bow of a lady, inflicting a severe wound. The little girl was taken to the West Kent General Hospital,

where she was an inpatient for some time, but was afterwards removed home, and she has since died from the effects of the wound. She was the only child of poor parents.
20/9/1868

Dramatic Torture.
TO THE EDITOR OF THE ERA.
Sir, – As one of the playgoing public, will you kindly permit me to call attention to the misery nightly inflicted on audiences, for the first hour of each night's performance, by the senseless trash exhibited from seven to eight, as a preliminary to pass away the time till the stall and box company arrive, as it would certainly be far better to begin at eight at once than to insult the assembly with such idiotic nonsense as I had the misfortune to witness at two of the London Theatres this week. Two such specimens I hope never to witness again. I know that the fashion of the time renders it necessary to keep back the real or intended entertainment till the booked parties arrive; and they, to their credit be it said, take very good care not to arrive till the introductory insipidity has been reluctantly swallowed by the old seven o'clockers. I have nothing to say against arranging the performance so as to suit the convenience of the high-class patrons of the Drama; but I must protest against treating the occupants of the pit and gallery with so-called farces, without wit, humour, or plot, which are not acted, but negligently slurred over, in a manner that would disgrace a strolling company in a country barn; and if Managers can do nothing better for the first hour, they had better do nothing at all. I am, Sir, your obedient servant, G.E. October 8th, 1868.
11/10/1868

SUICIDE THROUGH LOSS OF A SWEETHEART. – Yesterday morning a singular suicide was committed in Bethnal-green by a young man, whose sweetheart, a pretty girl, was about to leave England for Australia. The deceased was Charles McMillan, a bootmaker, living at 19, Emma-street, and he was in comfortable business circumstances. He was twenty-nine years of age, and for the last two years he was keeping company with a young woman, Alice Chapman. He was very fond of her, but a short time ago she told him that she was going to pay her passage to Australia. He implored her not to leave him alone in Bethnel-green. She refused to stop in England, and he became very sad. He had several meetings with her during the last few days, but all his entreaties were of no avail, and she declared that she would leave the country. Friday evening he said to his landlord, Mr Jones Roberts, "I am going away and you will never see me again. I owe you something, and I wish to settle with you before I go. I have ten pairs of boots made. Take them and sell them. You will also find two more at a beer shop. That will make twelve. In the back-yard I have a goat. Next Saturday week raffle him, and what the goat and boots will bring will pay you off. Good-bye." He then went upstairs to his room, and he was not seen alive afterwards. During Friday night he was heard walking about his room, and yesterday morning it was discovered that he had hanged himself.
25/10/1868

AN ACTRESS SHOT. – A little tragedy in real life was enacted a few evenings ago at the Swansea Theatre. It appeared that the coloured actor, named Mr Morgan Smith, had been engaged for a short time to take the principal characters in sensational dramas and tragic plays. During a desperate encounter in one of the pieces Mr Smith had been furnished with a loaded pistol, which had, unfortunately, been rather too heavily charged. When he had to fire at the heroine in the plot, the loud report startled the audience, and the unfortunate actress staggered back desperately wounded in real earnest. The wadding struck her on the arm, which rendered it necessary to have her removed to the infirmary, and there the poor woman will remain for some time. The lady's name is Miss Marie d'Alvéra.

THE LIABILITY OF PERSONS ENCOURAGING STREET MUSICIANS. – Three young Germans were charged at the Westminster Police-court with playing music after being required to move on. A lady

named Littleton, living in Eaton-place, said that for many years she and her husband had been much annoyed by street musicians, and had their peace and quiet continually disturbed, through the encouragement given them by a woman in the neighbourhood. The defendants were there on Friday, and she went out herself and motioned them away. They were about to do so, from perfectly understanding what she meant, when twopence was given them to continue playing, which they immediately did, and she gave them in charge. Proceedings had been taken some months ago against this person, but failed owing to a legal difficulty. Complainant was most anxious to be relieved from the annoyance, of which she daily complained. A German in attendance said that the defendants were going to be sent home on Monday. They had not been aware that the lady wanted them to move on. Mr Selfe said he should fine them 5s. each. The law was very clear upon this subject. If a person encouraged the men in playing after they were told to go away, he or she was liable to be prosecuted and fined the same as the street player. It was abominable that a person should be subjected to such a nuisance.
1/11/1868

LADIES who have had their Hair Destroyed by the use of Liquids for changing Brown Locks to Yellow, are respectfully informed that R. ALLISTON can greatly assist them in their dilemma, and apply an antidote to the bane from which they must necessarily have suffered. R. Alliston has the Largest, Best, and Cheapest Stock of Wigs and Head Dresses in London, 422, Strand.
8/11/1868

WANTED, to Purchase, TWO Second-hand BASKET HOBBY HORSES and ONE DONKEY, in good working order, with trappings, &c., in good condition. Address (by letter only), stating lowest price, to W.W., Post-office, 132, Jermyn-street, Haymarket.
13/12/1867

TO THE EDITOR OF THE ERA.
Sir, – In a notice of the performance at the Cabinet Theatre, that appeared in last week's *Era*, I am unjustly accused, not only of murdering the Queen's English, but of indulging in practices unbecoming a respectable amateur. I am confident the allegations arise from a strange mistake on the part of your splenetic reporter. Having received so many favourable notices at your hands, more especially in reference to my gentlemanly bearing on the stage, I am naturally indignant at such imputations as the following; indeed, my friends smiled commiseratingly when the writer averred that I picked my nose all the time, winked at my friends (I am happy to say I had none there) in front of the curtain, said *jined* for *joined*, and *everythink* for *everything*, flourished a filthy "dish-cloth" (I think that was the elegant expression), that my shoes were too large, &c. The "filthy dish-cloth" I held in my hand for a very short time was a *new* white handkerchief with a deep border of lace. I wore my own shoes, that fit me well, and I have yet to learn that stablemen's legs, in Sheridan's day, were cased in lute-string inexpressibles and white stockings. As to the "aspersions on my parts of speech," I can only say that the words "join" and "everything" are not to be found in Crabtree's part, and, as I gave the text *verbatim*, were certainly not uttered by me. Trusting to your impartiality for the insertion of this letter, I am, Sir, yours obediently, W. NICHOLLS.
27/12/1898

10
1869
EIGHT INCHES LESS THAN TOM THUMB

Theatrical Advertising.
A NUMBER of men, placard carriers in the employment of Mr Archibald Nagle, advertising agent, well known as the "bill-poster general," appeared at Bow-street yesterday to answer summonses charging them with carrying placards in the Strand, and thereby creating an obstruction, contrary to the provisions of the Traffic Regulation Act; and Mr Nagle himself was summoned for causing the other defendants to commit the alleged infraction of the law.

Inspector Thompson, of the E Division, stated that many complaints had lately been made of the obstruction caused by placard carriers walking in procession in the Strand. The placard carriers now charged had been found walking in the Strand with placards erected over their heads by means of an iron framework resting on their shoulders and strapped to their bodies.

A gentleman of imposing presence and florid complexion, who was stated to be a principal member of an eminent firm in the Strand, here came forward, and said that these proceedings had been taken chiefly in consequence of complaints made to the police by himself, on his own behalf and on that of his brother tradesmen in the Strand. Upon explanation, however, it appeared that his grievances arose from the misconduct of costermongers with their barrows, omnibus conductors, and others, and that he had really nothing to say against the theatrical bill carriers.

Mr Nagle said that he was not aware he was infringing the law, and the placards were so arranged that he did not think they could create any public inconvenience.

Mr Flowers was not quite so sure of that. He had found, when riding in the streets, that his horse was very apt to be frightened by seeing a man whose real height of from four to six feet was exaggerated, by the placard over his head, to an apparent height of ten or eleven feet, and still more by a procession of such figures. There was more force in the other part of Mr Nagle's defence. Probably he was not aware that he was infringing the law. He must, therefore, be informed what the law was. No person was permitted to carry any bill, placard, or picture about the streets, by way of advertisement, unless with the permission of the Commissioners of Police. Mr Nagle might think that his placard might be displayed in the street without public inconvenience. But he was not allowed to assume that. Let him submit it to the Commissioners, and ask their approval. Not wishing to impose a penalty if he could do otherwise, he (Mr Flowers) would adjourn the case for a fortnight. If in that interval any placards were sent out or carried by the same defendants, without the consent of the Commissioners, he should have to impose penalties. He hoped he should not be driven to do so, for he had great sympathy, as he hoped all right-minded men had, with these poor carriers, who, after all, were only trying to get an honest living. If the public were inconvenienced by the mode in which their work was conducted proper regulations must be made and enforced, but as far as it was in his power he should endeavour to enforce these regulations

with as little severity as possible towards these poor men. The employers, however, must be made to observe the laws. Similar summonses against Mr Critchley, Mr Barber, and of the men in their employment, were likwise adjourned for a fortnight on the same conditions.
31/1/1869

NOT POISON. – Ladies have avoided using almond flavour for fear of poison, but PRESTON and SONS, the Druggists of 88, Leadenhall Street, prepare a pure Essence that none need fear selling or using, being *guaranteed* free from prussic acid. It can be obtained of all Chemists and Grocers in bottles from 6d. Ask for PRESTON and SONS' Essence of Almonds.

AFTER DARK you can Purchase, opposite the ADELPHI THEATRE, First-rate Fitting TROUSERS from 13s. Come for FREDERICK PELTON'S Benefit, who trusts to be patronised by the Prince of WALES upon his return from the Pyramids. Doors open from Eight a.m. till Nine p.m. At FREDERICK PELTON'S CLOTHING DEPOT, 67, STRAND.

GEORGE NEWMAN and MISS MORTIMER, the Australian Duettists, and LITTLE FANNY, the Infant Nightingale, causing great Sensation in their New Burlesque, "Ye Scamps of London," the audience climbing over each others heads to witness the passing of the Railway Train. Agent, A. MAYNARD.

Hunkey Chunk. TOM GORDON, "De Original Comic Man ob Colour," concluded his Fourth highly successful engagement at the Cambridge, and appeared with his usual success at the ROTUNDA MUSIC HALL, LIVERPOOL, where all letters may be addressed.
21/2/1869

IMITATION OF THE CORNET.– A YOUNG LADY, who Imitates the above, would be happy to enter into an Engagement with Managers of Music Halls or others. Address (by letter), MISS TILLY PULLEN, 25, Rathbone-place, Oxford-street.
28/2/1869

A LEAP FOR LIFE; OR, THE SALAMANDER HORSE. MISS EDITH SANDFORD begs to contradict the rumour identifying her horse with that now performing at the Amphitheatre, under the name of "The Salamander Horse," the second title of one of her Equestrian Dramas, and which has doubtless arisen from the previous publicity given by her announcements.

MISS EDITH SANDFORD'S horse "ETNA" does not stand upon a pedestal, under an ingeniously contrived shower of fireworks; on the contrary she rides THROUGH THE FLAMES FROM THE STAGE TO THE FLIES. It would be premature to announce the other NUMEROUS AND STARTLING EFFECTS in her Equestrian Drama, which will shortly be produced AT A LONDON THEATRE, upon an Unprecedented Scale of Magnificence for a Short Season only, in consequence of her CONTINENTAL ENGAGEMENTS. All business communications to be addressed to Mr E. English, Dramatic Agent, 9, Garrick-street, Covent-garden.
4/4/1869

EXTRAORDINARY FOG IN LONDON. – On Thursday morning London was enveloped in a dense, yellowish black fog, which covered the great City as with the darkness of night. The atmosphere near the earth, at least on the north bank of the Thames, was, however, comparatively clear. There was but little of the thick mist of the common English fog; but the darkness overhung the City like a gigantic pall, and effectually obscured both sun and sky. It was most intense about eleven o'clock, but cleared away towards noon.
11/4/1869

SHOCKING OCCURRENCE IN A THEATRE. – On Monday evening Mr Charles Mathews performed at the Alnwick Theatre, and the house was crowded in every part. In the interval between the pieces a young man, named Robert Turner, attempted to pass over from the gallery and to enter the side boxes, but George Craster, a man employed for the purpose of keeping order, interfered. A struggle took place, and both men fell into the boxes, Craster undermost, with his arms round Turner's neck. Craster managed to rise, but Turner was unable to move, and was carried home, where he died shortly afterwards. Craster was immediately apprehended, and charged with having caused the death of Turner. He was brought before a Magistrate on Tuesday, and remanded until Saturday. On Tuesday evening an inquest was opened on the body of the deceased, who was aged thirty-two years, and was a joiner. Mr John Clifford, Manager of the Alnwick Theatre, stated that Craster was in his service. He was bill-poster and general deliverer and gallery check-taker. When preventing people passing over the top of the boxes on Monday evening, he was obeying his instructions. The inquest was adjourned.

AN UNREHEARSED SCENE. – On Tuesday se'nnight an accident occurred at the Theatre Royal, Birmingham, during the performance of Dion Boucicault's successful drama *After Dark*, which might have occasioned very serious, if not fatal, injuries to two of the performers engaged therein. The drama had progressed satisfactorily until the last scene of the third act, representing the Underground Railway, and Mr Edward Price (who is starring here as Old Tom) had just dragged Mr F. Gould (the Gordon Chumley of the piece) from the rails, when the train, propelled by a heavy counterweight, dashed on to the stage. Unfortunately the engine came in contact with that portion of the scene representing the railway arch, and was thrown violently on to the stage on its side, dragging down with it the signal post and lamp, the ponderous machine, weighing several hundredweights, falling close to the spot where the two characters were lying, and the funnel actually touching Mr Gould's head and taking off his wig. Fortunately, however, he sustained no more serious injury than a bruised cranium, while Mr Price escaped altogether unhurt.
18/4/1869

TO THE EDITOR OF THE ERA.
Sir, – In your last week's paper in the column "Original Correspondence," there is a letter from "Deaf as a Post," stating I have often played Shylock. I beg to say I never played the part. If he succeeds in finding the bill he mentions he will perceive he is not only "Deaf as a Post" but "Blind as a Bat." I am, Sir, yours, very truly, REBECCA POWELL, 52, Wellington-road, St John's-wood, N.W.

FALL OF A MUSIC HALL. – The new Adelphi Music Hall, Union-street, Oldham, which was opened a few months ago by the Oldham Philharmonic Society, fell down last Saturday morning, about nine o'clock, and has become a complete wreck. Friday night was fixed for the benefit of one of the *artistes* engaged, and as it was expected there would be a crowded house on the occasion, and it having been ascertained from an examination that the building was unsafe, the Managers very properly decided not to allow the performance to go forward in the building, which is calculated to hold 2,000 people. On Saturday morning, while the Lessee, Mr Seal, and some of the others connected with the place, were in the orchestra collecting their music, the east wall gave unmistakable evidence of its unsoundness, and they therefore rushed for the outside. They were only just in time, for Mr Seal was caught on the head by some of the falling building, but he is not seriously hurt. The east wall is completely down to the ground, and the roof and galleries are also destroyed. The cause of this catastrophe is the undermining of the foundations while excavating for the adjoining new buildings.
25/4/1869

LESSEE OF THE JARROW THEATRE IN TROUBLE. – Yesterday, at the South Shields County Petty Sessions, William Spencer Jones, who a short while ago had the Jarrow Theatre, was summoned by Mary Montague, one of the actresses engaged by him, for having on Saturday last committed an unprovoked and brutal assault upon her. The defendant did not answer to the summons, and the Magistrates heard the case in his absence. Complainant said when they were rehearsing a piece on Saturday Mrs Jones (defendant's wife) came up to her and asked her if she would take a certain part in the piece, but witness declined, as she said she was not engaged to play that line. On Miss Montague refusing to play the part, Mrs Jones seized her by the hair and dragged her across the stage to where defendant was, and they then both endeavoured to throw her down some stairs. Mrs Jones, failing in that, caught complainant in her arms and tossed her to Jones, saying, "Give it to her," whereupon Jones swung his arm round her, and getting her head in his left arm, commenced to batter her face with his fist. He struck her several severe blows under the chin and knocked seven of her teeth out. She thought Jones was going to kill her, and "she gave herself to God," saying, "Lord, take my soul." When defendant relaxed hold of her her jaws were locked, and it took her two hands before she could open her mouth, and when she did so several teeth fell out. Defendant had since ran away, but had property in Tyne Dock. The Magistrates considered the case a very bad one, and imposed a fine of £5 and costs, complainant to receive half of the fine. – *Newcastle Daily Chronicle*, April 28th.

THE ADVERTISER is desirous of placing his little DAUGHTER, aged eight years, with a Stage Manager or Dramatic Trainer, with whom she could likewise receive instruction in the usual branches of a plain education. Address, stating on what terms this could be arranged, ARTIST, 31, Torwood-street, Torquay.
2/5/1869

THE PATENT SAFETY SELF-LIGHTING CIGAR. – The Messrs R.M. Bennett and Co., cigar merchants, of the Octagon, Plymouth, are the holders of a very admirable patent in the manufacture of cigars. This invention renders the smoker completely independent of vesuvians or any other kind of light. The end of the "Allomette" cigar is covered with a preparation, of which powdered charcoal is the foundation. Round each cigar is a small paper band. On this is a small piece of another composition, and by passing the end of the cigar over this spot instant ignition takes place. There is no odour to interfere with the smoker's enjoyment, and an even light is at once secured. The preparation will only ignite on the band, so that no danger can possibly exist. Among the many advantages of this patent must be reckoned the safety from chances of fire which it secures. The light does not drop about, and it is well known that fragments from burning fusees have caused many a serious conflagration.

A HOUSE BLOWN UP BY A WOMAN. – On Friday night Langley, a gunpowder agent, of Hanley, sent five hundredweight of powder to John Espley, a colliery contractor, of Newcastle-under-Lyme. The carter placed the powder in a coach-house, and went to tell Espley that it had arrived. Within ten minutes Mrs Espley fired the powder. The building was totally destroyed. She herself was buried in the ruins. A beam fell over her chest. The woman is still alive, but frightfully injured. Domestic unhappiness is said to be the cause of the act. A man passing was also injured on the head, and taken to the infirmary.
9/5/1869

TO THE EDITOR OF THE ERA. – Sir, will you permit the following to appear in your paper: – "In writing letters on the stage actors and actresses are in the habit of writing much faster than ever any man or woman had the fortune of being taught; in fact, to watch them (I do not mean to say all do), some appear to make *lines* across the paper. Now, as a regular playgoer, let me give you my opinion, and that is that the more trifling the circumstance the more it is noticed. Therefore, ladies and gentlemen, let me persuade you to think that letter writing is not like the telegraph system, because, no doubt, as you are all aware, every eye in the house is watching, like a cat would a mouse, for the least thing to make of;

therefore, try and subdue this evil before it gets a general remark that he or she wrote as all actors and actresses generally do, quite out of reason." I hope that by inserting this note it will have the effect I wish, that of subduing a great stage evil. I am, Sir, yours truly, W.G., Finsbury, May 18th.

REMARKABLE THEATRICAL FEAT. – As an illustration of the modern railway facilities afforded the Theatrical Profession we may mention that a few evening since Mr Henry Montgomery, of the Prince of Wales Theatre, played in the first piece, *A Winning Hazard*, at Tottenham-street, London, and the same night acted Dame Martha, at Dover, in Burnand's burlesque of *Alonzo the Brave*, the performances being for the benefit of a local charity, and principally sustained by the officers of the 4th King's Own. The same extraordinary feat was accomplished by Mr Montgomery the following night, the two Theatres being ninety miles apart.

AN UNREHEARSED SENSATION SCENE AT ASTLEY'S. – During the performance of *The Battle of Waterloo* on Thursday night, in the course of the taking of the Bridge of Marchiennes, which concludes the first act, one of the horses became unmanageable, and, after several plunges, backed into the centre of the orchestra, carrying away the conductor, and injuring several members of the band, one of whom, Mr Parkin (clarinet player), now lies in the hospital of the Fusilier Guards with a fractured collar bone. Some valuable instruments were likewise destroyed, though, strange to say, neither the horse nor its rider was hurt. Mr Brandon Ellis appealed to the indulgence and patience of the audience, while the debris of music and instruments was collected, and order being at length restored, the majority of the band resumed their places, a cordial greeting being accorded to Mr William Corri, the conductor, over whom the horse had passed, whom every one feared to have been buried under the falling horse, but who had almost miraculously escaped with only some slight scratches. The performance then proceeded without interruption.
23/5/1869

ESCAPE OF "THE CAPTIVE" BALLOON. – The "Captive Balloon," at Ashburnham-park, Chelsea, while no one was in the car, broke loose from its moorings on Tuesday afternoon, and sailed away in a north-westerly direction. It passed over Watford and Tring, and a little to the north of Aylesbury, crossing the Aylesbury and Buckingham line of railway at Grandborough-road. About this place the car was very near the earth, and the 9-inch cable, which snapped when the balloon broke from its fastening, dragged the ground several times. It was at last caught in a large elm tree at Botolph Claydon, Buckinghamshire, a farm belonging to Sir Harry Verney. Some fifty or sixty persons who had followed the balloon secured it by lashing the ropes round the trunks of the adjoining trees. Sir Harry Verney and Colonel Pratt were soon on the spot, and under their directions precautions were taken to prevent it being injured.
30/5/1869

The BABIES at the ALFRED THEATRE.
IN years to come the notice which lately appeared at the Alfred Theatre will be looked upon as a curious record of theatrical life. We give the "Babies' Cloak Room" handbill in full, as such quaint productions deserve to become matters of dramatic history. The bill runs as follows: –

ROYAL ALFRED THEATRE. – NOTICE. – Great annoyance having being caused during the Performance by the Crying of Infants, the Management has determined upon refusing admittance to any Children under Five years of age; but, in order to prevent the disappointment to Mothers consequent on such a regulation, a large room will be set apart as a BABIES' CLOAK ROOM, in which Children can be left the entire Evening for 2d. each. A Staff of Nurses will be in attendance, and every requisite in the shape of Feeding Bottles, Milk, &c., provided without extra charge. May 17, 1869.

The extremely liberal, not to say generous, offer of the Management was accepted by many matrons of Marylebone, who thankfully paid their twopence, and revelled in the Drama, while their offspring

kicked and screamed, or tranquilly slumbered in the arms of the "Staff of Nurses." One pleasant little surprise was, however, in store for the thoughtful rulers of the Alfred Theatre, and their opinion of the maternal instinct of the Paddingtonian mothers must now be small indeed. To leave the babies in the "large room" and forget to call for them, was the easiest thing in the world; and the price of admission to the Alfred Theatre, with twopence extra for feeding bottles and milk, was evidently looked upon as a cheap mode of narrowing the domestic circle. THREE living proofs of gratitude to the Management have been left in the cloak-room, and from thence to the parish workhouse is the next journey these little unfortunates will take.
6/6/1869

Disturbance at a Music Hall.

William Edwards and Julia Edwards, vocalists, were placed at the Southwark-police bar, before Mr Partridge, charged with creating a disturbance at the Star Music Hall, Neckinger-road, Bermondsey.

Mr Slater, the Manager, said that the prisoners, who were unknown to him, visited their establishment, and got into a conversation with a Mrs Kent, who had her children with her, and at the close of the performances they accompanied her to the parlour of the Hotel. Mrs Kent called him, and asked him if it was right of her to to give the prisoners 7s. 6d. as singers at their Hall. He told her that the prisoners were not connected with their establishment, and she had better get her money back. The prisoners became very violent, and witness was compelled to eject them and give them into custody.

In cross-examination witness said that Mrs Kent paid for several bottles of champagne, with which she treated the prisoners and other people near her. He had six or seven glasses, but he was perfectly sober.

Georgina Kent, the wife of a grocer, said she went to the Music Hall with her children, when the prisoners, who sat behind her, took notice of one of the girls and nursed her. She accordingly treated them to champagne, and as they said they were singers and going to have a benefit she handed them 7s. 6d. They had more champagne, and on her telling Mr Slater what she had done a disturbance took place. They all drank a good deal of champagne, but they were not drunk.

Mr Partridge observed that the disturbance was brought on by Mrs Kent and the champagne, and as the prisoners had been locked up all night he should discharge them.

THE NOVELTY OF THE DAY. C.A. BOOTH, the Renowned Champion, surnamed the VELOCIPEDIAN DUCROW!
"A STARTLING AND ALMOST INCREDIBLE PERFORMANCE. – Mr C.A. Booth goes through his astounding and marvellous evolutions on the Velocipede, performing elegant and truly astounding feats on his Iron Steed, similar to those executed by the famous Mons. Ducrow when on a bare-backed horse, the only difference being that the Velocipedist actually performs all the daring feats of the renowned Andrew Ducrow on the Velocipede, in addition to performing on a musical instrument, and doing numerous magical tricks, whilst whirling himself with the rapidity of lighting round the stage." – Astley's, Theatre Royal, May 17th, 1869.
"VELOCIPEDE TRAVELLING EXTRAORDINARY. – On Wednesday, the 14th inst., Mr Charles Albert Booth (Champion of Skating) performed the distance from London to Brighton in seven and a half hours, this being the quickest journey over that route by two hours. Mr Booth arrived in Brighton in time to have a bath, take dinner, and catch the last train to town, when he was received and congratulated by his numerous friends on the success of his long journey." – Vide *Standard and Blue Budget*, April 17th, 1869.
13/6/1869

TO THE EDITOR OF THE ERA.
Mdme. Adelina Patti.
Sir, – On Friday (25th ult.) the opera of the *Figlia del Reggimento*, with Mdme. Adelina Patti in it, and the operetta of *Don Bucefalo*, were duly announced in all the newspapers, and at all the libraries, at the box office, &c., up to the very hour of opening the doors. After the Royal Italian Opera was opened there was still no notice whatever, outside the walls of the Theatre, announcing any change of performance; but on entering the house, after numerous parties had sent their carriages away, and entered the house under the firm belief that they were to hear Patti in the *Figlia*, notices were found posted in the corridors to the effect that Mdme. Patti was suffering from a severe hoarseness which rendered her totally unable to sing, and that consequently the directors were compelled to substitute the opera of the *Huguenots*, which was accordingly given, with Tietiens, and not another decent performer in it; and with that one exception it was disgracefully performed.

Everybody would naturally pity Mdme. Patti with her hoarseness, but not so much when they learned next morning, by that infallible *enfant terrible*, the *Court Circular*, not only that the Marquis and Marquise de Caux were guests of their Royal Highnesses the Prince and Princess of Wales at Marlborough House, but that Mdme. Patti sang two beautiful airs at the said concert most divinely, and that the hoarseness which so suddenly prevailed in Bow-street, Covent-garden, no less suddenly disappeared in Pall-mall. In fact, a friend of mine, who had the honour of being present at the concert, informed me that she never heard Patti sing better!

Now although I quite understand how delighted the Prince of Wales may have been to have Mdme. Patti among his guests, and how charmed the fair Marquise must have been to assist at so historical a scene, yet I must ask whether the proceedings at the Royal Italian Opera were quite fair on the public? Will anybody believe for one moment that Messrs Gye and Mapleson did not perfectly well know that Mdme. Patti was invited both as a guest and a singer at the concert at Marlborough House hours and hours before the opening of the doors of their Theatre, or that they had not deliberately let the fair prima donna off her previous engagement? Her name was in the programme of the Concert at Marlborough House; and the pieces that she was to sing must have been selected, at latest, the night before. Then why willfully deceive the public up to the very last, and why tell the public "the thing which was not?" For the hoarseness "was not."

This is written on behalf of several persons, ladies especially, who had come from the country on purpose to hear Patti, and who sent their carriages away because no notice of a change was posted outside the walls of the Theatre, so that to have their money back was out of the question. I am, Sir, yours, &c., AN M.P.
4/7/1869

SAM BAGNELL has SOLD the COPYRIGHT of the following SONGS to Mr D'Alcorne and Crew: – "Who'll Buy My Violets," "Silver Herring," "Cackle Cackle," and "Naughty Miss Ricketts." Send stamps.

To Managers of *Fetes*, Galas, &c. THE LITTLE VELOCIPEDIAN WONDERS. MASTER EDWARD BARBER (Eight Years of age), Champion Boy Rider, and Winner of the Silver Cup, at the Agricultural Hall, Saturday, July 24th, against Youths of Sixteen Years, appears every Evening in his magnificent dress as the young Prince Imperial, on his Presentation Bicycle; also MISS NELLY SMITH (aged Ten), on a Bicycle, Side Saddle, in Riding Habit. For terms, apply to the Director of the Velocipedian Cirque, Agricultural Hall, Islington. Size of stage immaterial.
1/8/1869

TO THE EDITOR OF THE ERA.
Sir, – On Monday, accompanied by three young ladies and three children, I took excursion tickets for Brighton. On approaching the barrier where tickets are cut, I was saluted with "Can't pass with that – must book that there," the remark applying to a small black bag I had in my hand. Seeing others in the same predicament, and the time for the departure of the train being near, I deposited the offending bag in the appointed place, and saw it duly labelled with my name. Upon my arrival at Brighton, I was told it would come down by the next train, and, after about an hour's delay, the bag was handed to me with a request to sign my name and demand for 8d. Now, Sir, considering the said bag only contained a bottle of wine and one pound of tea, I can't help thinking that I have been imposed upon. I am, &c., C.W.
15/8/1869

TO THE EDITOR OF THE ERA.
Sir, – On arriving at York on Sunday morning last, at ten o'clock, two of us went into a little unassuming-looking coffee-house for the purpose of getting breakfast; we had it, and I paid for it *through the nose*. One cup of coffee, a small piece of bacon, and two eggs each. Upon the conclusion of this sumptuous meal we were charged *three shillings and fourpence*. Surely, Sir, this is exorbitant in the extreme, and greatly exceeds the charge of a first-class hotel. The Provincial branch of the Profession suffers enough already, from heavy railway fares, *long* journeys, and *short* engagements; we don't want over-reaching eating-house keepers down upon us. May I give my brother Professionals a suggestion. Do as I intend for the future on long journeys, carry your *own* provender with you. I remain, yours truly, FRANK W. EGERTON.

EXTRAORDINARY SWARM OF LADYBIRDS. – Ramsgate on Sunday was visited by a vast swarm of ladybirds. They filled the air and covered the earth at every conceivable point. Their number was greatest about noon, when they were to be seen on projecting corners of houses, collected so as to form one red patch. Later in the day the air got somewhat thinned of them, owing to the traffic of the streets and the destruction which they met with. The streets then presented a peculiar appearance. The number of these bodies strewn about caused the roads to look as though newly gravelled. It is a somewhat curious fact that these insects paid Ramsgate and its neighbourhood a visit in August, 1849, in great numbers, upon which occasion the only noticeable effect of their visit was the extinction of the *aphides*, which was of great advantage to the hop crop. The south side of the Thames has also had a visit of thousands of ladybirds, especially Balham, Tooting, and Streatham.

FOR SALE, FIVE SCENES, Three Pairs of Wings, Green Baize Drop Curtain, Proscenium, Landscapes, a Large Tree, including all Stage requisites, price £35 for the whole, or £30 without Proscenium. The above is nearly New, and of First-Class Paintings. Apply, G.W. REE, Belle Vue Inn, Aberdare.
22/8/1869

Coloured Silk Socks – A Warning.
Sir, – The following facts may be useful to others. After having worn, for about a fortnight, silk socks of different colours, I felt my feet itching, and saw little pimples come out on the skin. Heat, and increased itching, produced a most disagreeable sensation, which became worse every day. The pimples began to come out in regular blisters, and on the sixth day the feet were greatly swollen all round, and all covered with blisters just as if they had been burnt by fire. The pains were also the same. The soles of the feet were particularly bad, and for twelve days after that I was laid up. During the first five or six days I had applications, composed of oily ingredients, put on, and after that, rye flour, and then bismuth and flour. After twelve days I found the blisters began to dry up, and only on the twenty-first day after it first appeared could I venture to put on a boot again and walk a little. The colours particularly dangerous are all red shades, scarlet, brown, and yellow; all in which "coraline" is to be found. I am, &c., A SUFFERER.

The Era contains several accounts of actors having their feet poisoned by scarlet tights.

DETECTIVES OUTWITTED BY AN ACTOR. – A very amusing scene occurred at Pablo's Circus, at Rochdale, the other evening, in the presence of an audience of about 2,000 persons. The performance was concluded with the old and familiar farce entitled *The Frolic*. Mr Hickey, in the piece, represented a drunken countryman, and so well did his dress and manner correspond with that character that two detectives were deceived.

As this week is the season of the Rochdale wakes, old and experienced officers are selected out to act as detectives on account of the town being infested on such occasions by the light-fingered fraternity, and on the evening in question two officers were present at the Circus dressed in plain clothes. The farce had opened, and Mr Sweeny, acting as Clown, was frolicking on horseback, when Hickey, in true Bacchanalian style, stumbled from the gallery into the ring and demanded a ride, saying that the Clown had promised it for a quart of ale. A pretended squabble ensued between the supposed countryman, the ring-master, and the manager, Mr Henry Montague, when the two latter, according to the farce, quickly called for the assistance of the police to eject the supposed countryman. To the surprise of the performers and some of the audience, two police officers rushed into the ring, declaring that they could not permit a drunken man to interfere with the progress of the performance, collared him, and although Hickey loudly protested that he was not drunk, but acting the character, dragged him out of the Circus amidst protracted roars of laughter. Mr Pablo and Mr Montague followed the two officers out of the Circus and explained the plot of the piece to the police, who then gave up their charge and laughed heartily at their promptitude and the way they had been outwitted.
29/8/1869

SERIOUS CHARGE. – A person known as Professor Risley, the Proprietor of the "Royal Japanese *Troupe*," was on Wednesday brought up in custody at Marlborough-street, charged with assaulting a little girl eleven years of age, Maria Mason by name. The case for the prosecution is that the child, whilst passing through Leicester-square and one or two of the neighbouring thoroughfares, was several times molested by the prisoner, who laid hold of her, and endeavoured to force her into places against her will. At length the child took refuge in a house in Greek-street, and the principal witness, Mr Hales, a reporter, who had watched the prisoner from the commencement, gave information to the police. Upon being questioned, he gave the name of Ricardo, and his address as the Surrey Theatre. The child was not present on Wednesday to give evidence, but Mr Knox decided that the charge must be proceeded with. At the close of the hearing the prisoner was remanded, the Magistrate refusing bail, as of late there had been so many compromises of serious cases at that court. On Thursday the hearing was resumed, when the evidence of the little girl, Mason, was taken in support of the prosecution, which corroborated all Mr Hales' statements. Mr Knox decided that he could not keep the case from the consideration of a Jury, and in sending the defendant for trial, consented to take bail, himself in £400, and two sureties in £200 each.

LONDON PAVILION. – Triumphant Success of THE GILLENO FAMILY. MISS CARLOTTA GILLENO creates quite a sensation nightly in her Graceful and Daring High Rope Performances, including her Extraordinary Feats with a Common Chair, and the Wonderful Act of running with her Brother on her shoulders both up and down the whole length of the Hall, surpasses all performances of the kind ever witnessed.
5/9/1869

To Licensed Victuallers and Music Hall Proprietors. THE SMALLEST MAN in the World would be happy to make arrangements to Serve behind a Bar, or to Appear at any Music Hall. In both capacities he would be very attractive. He is Thirty-two Years of Age, and only Thirty Inches High (Eight Inches

less than Tom Thumb). Well up in the English Language and Bar and Concert Hall Business. Letters to be addressed to CHE MAH, 19, Trafalgar-street, Leeds.
12/9/1869

WANTED, a DWARF, Male or Female, not Deformed, to walk about a Waxworks Exhibition and Sculpture Galleries to Sell Catalogues. Must be able to converse. Address, with full particulars as to Age, Height, &c., to W. ALLSOP, Teutonic Hall, Lime-street, Liverpool.
19/9/1869

Hamlet "Again" Murdered.
TO THE EDITOR OF THE ERA.
Sir, – Perhaps some of your readers would be interested in the following particulars of what must be a unique performance of *Hamlet*, which took place in one of the leading cities of the west of England on Wednesday, the 22nd ult., by what the bills called a double company, though, when they read the sequel, they will say it should have been called a doubling company.

One female took the characters of Marcellus, Guildenstern, Player Queen, and Osric; another took Bernardo and Horatio during the Churchyard Scene. As to the men, one was Horatio, then, Rosencrantz, spoke the prologue, and was Lucianus in the Play Scene, was Second Gravedigger, and then Horatio again. The Ghost, First Player, and Priest were got through by another, Polonius and First Gravedigger by another.

Mr Chatterton, Mr Barry Sullivan, and other managers in London, who produce the legitimate drama, should surely not allow the Provinces to possess such *versatile talent* without trying to induce it to come to London.

But seriously, more abominable imitations of humanity, or a more decided burlesque of Shakespeare's sublime play, it would be difficult to see.

The parties engaged in the performance were seemingly trying to prevent the audience from finding out whether or not it was really Shakespeare's *Hamlet* they were seeing, as the Queen persisted in calling her son Ham*lut*; and Laertes was a little disguised in liquor. Yours truly, "PETER QUINCE."
3/10/1869

LEEDS – LLOYD'S ARMS CONCERT HALL, KIRKSTALL-ROAD. WANTED, a COLOURED LADY PIANIST, to play a few Nights a week. To board and live and assist in the house. Address, stating lowest terms, Mr SAMUEL THORNTON, Proprietor, as above.
24/10/1869

THE ONE THING NEEDFUL TO PROFESSIONALS. – Now Publishing, a Simple and Correct POCKET GUIDE, showing, without half a minute's trouble, the distance from any one to any other of the principal Towns in England and Scotland where there are Theatres and Music Halls, with a useful Diary, by which any Professional can see at a glance his or her Engagements and Vacant Dates, &c. Also a Register of First-class Apartments in the said Towns suitable to Professionals. All Parties wishing to have their Apartments entered in the Register and Guide can do so by applying at once to Messrs FIELD and WHITE, 15, Fletcher-gate, Nottingham. Terms for Advertising, One Shilling per Year.

Mr Toole Paying for Admission to his own Performance.
IT is seldom we read of an actor being required to pay for admission to his own entertainment. Yet such was the case with Mr Toole on Saturday afternoon. Shortly before the Volunteer Bazaar closed at four o'clock, the popular comedian paid a visit to the Drill Hall. He was barely within the doors when his identity was discovered, and he was surrounded by the "fairy" stall-keepers, who fairly swindled him out of several pounds in lottery tickets for sofa blankets, cushions, cosies, slippers, smoking caps, and all the other paraphernalia sold at fancy bazaars.

But Mr Toole was not to be let off with a simple expenditure of money. Col. Sandeman, hearing that he was in the Hall, came and asked him to give an entertainment of some kind, if only for a few minutes. The gallant Colonel would take no denial, and Mr Toole, though totally at a loss to know how he would manage to entertain an audience on so short a notice, consented with characteristic good humour. The announcement was, therefore, made in the large Hall that Mr Toole would give an entertainment in the ante-room, the price of admission being fixed at one shilling. Ladies at once took their places at the doors to collect the money, and so hurriedly was the whole affair gone about that Mr Toole had not time to get in. Immediately the announcement was made, there was a rush to the doors, and it was soon seen that there was to be "a crowded house." Of course, Mr Toole expected to get in without paying. But no – the lady at the door was inexorable, and, before getting admission he had to pay his shilling, like the rest of the audience. The room was crowded in a few moments; and the company could not have numbered fewer than one hundred and fifty persons – representing a sum of between seven and eight pounds contributed to the funds of the Bazaar. If Mr Toole had had the time at his disposal, he would have been glad to have given two or three separate performances in behalf of the Volunteers. As it was, the entertainment was a great success, and the eminent comedian was intensely tickled at the idea of having to pay a shilling to see Toole!

A SET OF TEETH IN COURT. – On Wednesday, at the Kendal County Court, a young man sued Messrs Scales Brothers of that town, dentists, to recover £2, paid to the defendants for a set of new teeth which would not fit, though three sets had been made. Plaintiff – Why, your Honour, they would not stick up; they were like a cradle in my mouth. They rocked here and there, and there and here. Mr Henry Scales – The fact is, your Honour, the plaintiff has not a single tooth in his lower jaw to support the new ones. The teeth were here handed into court. On seeing them the plaintiff cried in a loud voice, "They are not the teeth; I'll swear they're not the teeth." Mr Scales – And I'll swear they are. Here the plaintiff and the defendant confronted one another sternly, the plaintiff holding out the teeth at arm's length, and surveying them with mingled expressions of wonder and awe. The Judge – Well, try if they will fit your particular case. The plaintiff here opened his mouth, and was going to perform the experiment literally in open court, when the Judge interposed and told the plaintiff to retire to a more suitable place. The parties retired accordingly, and nothing further had been heard of them when the Court rose. To lend an additional element to the picturesque appearance of the Court, it may be added that the chamber of justice was hung with the scenery for the opera of *Norma*, the apartment having been let to a company of lyric actors.
31/10/1869

Gymnastic Sensations.
TO THE EDITOR OF THE ERA.
Sir, – Having seen a very flaming advertisement announcing that a certain lady gymnast would shortly appear, and cross a tight-rope upon a velocipede, the wheels of which were *without grooves*, I was induced to pay a visit to the Music Hall in question, believing that a performance of the kind described would be well repaid, especially as I found that Blondin was performing the same feat *with grooved wheels*, which fact he candidly tells you in his advertisements. Well, on Saturday evening I watched very carefully the performance on the rope of the lady, where, true, she did cross the rope on a velocipede, but the wheels of which were so constructed that a portion of the rope was invisible in consequence of the wheels being so grooved as actually to nearly cover it, besides which a male performer (her partner) hangs on a sort of trapeze suspended from the velocipede, which acts as a counter balance, and renders locomotion quite as simple as if on *terra firma*. Now, I have no wish in any way whatever to try and damage the fair lady's performance, which is decidedly novel, while her other feats are very clever and well worth a visit to see; but I say that it is quite time these exaggerations in

catering for the public amusement should be exposed. Trusting you will insert this in your next, I remain, yours obediently, GYMNAST.
14/11/1869

AN IMPUDENT BARMAN.
STONE v. PAXMAN. – The plaintiff in this action was a barman and potman, formerly in the employ of Mr Alfred Paxman, of the Blackstock Park Hotel, Seven Sisters-road, Holloway, and he sued the defendant in the Clerkenwell County Court for 15s. wages. The defendant did not not appear.

Plaintiff stated that he was engaged by defendant on the 16th of July last as a potman and barman, at 8s. per week wages. He only remained in defendant's employ thirteen days. On the 29th July, about four o'clock in the afternoon, plaintiff was discovered by defendant in the cellar drinking half-a-quartern of brandy. The brandy belonged to defendant, who called a policeman and had plaintiff locked up. Plaintiff was taken before the Magistrate at the Clerkenwell Police-court, and was sentenced to two months' imprisonment. After he came out of prison he went for his box, and on applying for his wages defendant refused to give it to him.

His Honour – How much do you think I am going to give you? Plaintiff – I don't know, your Honour.
His Honour – Nothing at all.
Plaintiff said if all barmen were treated in the same way he had been, there would soon be none at all.
His Honour – Then all I can say is they are a bad lot. Did you ever go to school? Plaintiff said he had.
His Honour – Did they teach you there to drink your master's brandy? Plaintiff said he was not taught anything about that.
His Honour – But they taught you to keep your hands from picking and stealing. Don't you think you deserved the two months' imprisonment? Plaintiff said he did not think he did.
His Honour – Well, I do, and the sooner you are out of this court the better.
Judgement for defendant.

Special Engagement of PROFESSOR BROWN on the BICYCLE at the CANTERBURY HALL, Saturday, November 27th, who will cut a sheep in half with a sword, and will shave himself, get his meal, while riding on the Bicycle, and a great many other Tricks too numerous to mention. Must be seen to be believed.
28/11/1869

THE GHOST OF "HAMLET'S" FATHER. – The *Morning Post*, in noticing the performance of *Hamlet* at the Princess's Theatre, says: – "At the close of the first act there was, for the first time within our memory, a call for the Ghost (could the ghosts of our fathers have heard it, what *would* they have said?); and, what's more, he 'took the call,' as the actors say, and made for the footlights amid the huzzas of the spectators. Spirits may now be summoned from the vasty deep, and the chances are that they will come. After this crowning absurdity of the call system, *la fin du monde*."
5/12/1869

The Unreality of Realistic Scene Painting.
TO THE EDITOR OF THE ERA.
Sir, – It is a curious fact, which I believe none of the theatrical critics have called attention to, that notwithstanding the rage for realism on the stage, and the expense to which Managers go in ministering to it, few of the great scenes of the realistic dramas are correct representations of the localities they are intended to bring before the eye of the spectator. That I may not be accused of hypercriticism, I will mention three remarkable instances of this defect.

In *Lost at Sea*, the scene in which Kate is saved from suicide represents the steamboat pier at Hungerford in the foreground, with the railway bridge springing from the left-hand side. This view of the bridge can be obtained only by standing in a position in which Westminster-bridge cannot be seen;

yet that bridge is made visible in the scene under Charing Cross-bridge – that is, where Waterloo-bridge ought to be. The view would be correct if taken from the Surrey side, as the previous scene – the arch under the Waterloo-road – would lead the spectator to suppose it had been; but there is no pier on that side.

The last scene of *Land Rats and Water Rats* was defective in a similar way. The Thames Embankment works (then in progress) were built up in the foreground, and Westminster-bridge was represented crossing diagonally from left to right, with the river facade of the Houses of Parliament seen through the arches. Such a view would of course only be obtained from the Surrey side, to which the artist seemed to have transferred the embankment works then lately commenced below the bridge on the Westminster side.

My third example was the scene in *Life in Lambeth* – the Victoria version of *The Streets of London* – described in the bills as Boneboiler's-alley. That odoriferous locality, now swept away by the march of improvement, was on the south-side of Upper Fore-street, and consequently at right angles with the river, so that a person looking at it from the position of the spectator in the Theatre would have his back to the river. Yet the scene showed the clock tower of the Houses of Parliament in the distance!

With so much striving after realism as we have seen in the dramas mentioned, and in *After Dark*, *Formosa*, &c., it seems strange that Managers should neglect the accessories of the illusion that they are at so much pains to produce to the extent often witnessed. I saw, a few evenings ago, a banker's drawing-room, the carpet of which did not cover the floor; a room without a single article of furniture, to sustain the idea of its being occupied; and a couple of liveried servants carrying a table off the stage at the close of a scene representing the home of a poor man! These defects were exhibited in one piece at a Theatre in the Strand which I need not name, as the penetration of your readers will suffice. DRAMATICUS.

Envy, Malice, or Jealousy. £100 REWARD. – In consequence of the legitimate success of HASSAN, "The Gorilla Chief," or Man Monkey, at Astley's, now under the direction of the Leviathan Manager, Mr E.T. Smith, some ill-disposed person attempted the life of the poor animal by throwing a poisoned orange to him at the finish of his performances; but as Mr Van Hare, his cautious protector, never allowing Hassan to have anything but from his own hands, their atrocious intentions were defeated. The above reward will be paid on conviction of the offender by VAN HARE, 64, Stafford-place, Buckingham Palace.
19/12/1869

SELF "PUFFING." – In the name of common decency we must renew our protest against the practice which which has grown up of late years at some of our London Theatres of puffing the actors in the play-bills. Whether the puffs in question originate with the Management or are quoted from other sources the offence against good taste is equally flagrant. It is an affront to the audience, whose favourable judgement is to be thus clumsily forestalled; and it is an insult to any actors who have a proper sense of what is due to their own dignity and that of their Profession. Nothing, surely, can be more offensive to an actress of Mrs Lander's distinction than to read in the Lyceum house play-bill that "Mrs Lander is as good an artist as ever lived," and that "her name has long been associated with the highest dramatic triumphs, and is a very potent magnet to the lovers of art." To find oneself lauded in this fantastic strain, side by side with enconiums on "fancy soap," "knife polish," "Manilla cigars," "cherry tooth-paste," and "medicine for the people," must indeed be a sore trial to an actor worthy of the name. – *Morning Post*, December 20th.
26/12/1869

11
1870
I'LL GIVE UP ACTING AND TRY THE POLICE TRICK

ALARMING EXPLOSION AND PANIC IN A MUSIC HALL.
During the performance of the Pantomime at the Southminster Music Hall, at Edinburgh, on Saturday night, an explosion occurred, which, while fortunately attended with no serious results, was productive of much alarm among the audience. A tremendous report shook the building from floor to rooftree. At the same instant a thick cloud of dust and smoke rose over the stage, and a moment later the whole house was in darkness, the lights having all been blown out. A panic seized the audience, and, amid the half-suppressed screams of the females, a rush was made to the doors. To make matters worse, when the doors were reached they were found to be blockaded by a crowd from the outside, who, attracted by the noise, were pressing in to see what had happened. Disastrous consequences seemed inevitable, when a voice from the stage was heard to call out through the darkness, "Keep your seats, gentlemen; there is no danger." Another minute and a light was brought, and the Proprietor made his appearance on stage. He assured the audience that there was no cause for alarm, and, reminding them of the recent melancholy occurrence at Bristol, pointed out that, even if a serious accident had taken place, there was nothing worse they could do than make a wild rush to the doors. By the time he concluded the house had been lighted up again, and in a few minutes more the air began to get cleared of the gas and dust with which it was filled. Confidence being at length completely restored to the audience, the performers were recalled and the Pantomime proceeded with as if nothing had occurred.

The accident, which thus so narrowly missed a disastrous termination, is understood to have been caused by the bursting of two bags of gas, which were being used for the production of the oxy-hydrogen light. The bags were made of a preparation of vulcanite, and contained each some six or seven cubic feet of gas. One of the bags held oxygen, and the other hydrogen; and it is supposed that they had burst in consequence of over-pressure. The gas, thus being released, must have come in contact with some gas jet or other flame, when the oxygen and hydrogen having got mixed in due proportion, the explosion was the result. The violent nature of the shock will be understood when it is stated that it made the whole building vibrate, and that hardly a whole pane of glass has been left in any of the windows.
16/1/1870

SELDOM has a marriage in Portsmouth caused such a sensation as one which took place at the Wesleyan Chapel, Arundel Street, Landport, on Monday morning (21st ult.). The bridegroom was Sumjoo, one of a troupe of three performing Indians, at present fulfilling an engagement with Mr William Brown, of the South of England Music Hall, and the bride was Miss Elvina Hall, daughter of Mr Hall, chiropodist, of the High Street. On Saturday last posters were issued from the Music Hall announcing the marriage, and the result was that long before eleven o'clock, the hour announced for the ceremony to take place, the

chapel was besieged with crowds of persons anxious to obtain admission to witness the proceedings. The street was thronged with people, and the traffic was suspended for some considerable time. Shortly before eleven the wedding party arrived in two carriages drawn by greys, and was well received by the crowd. The bridegroom was dressed in full English costume, as were also the other members of the troupe. After the ceremony the party returned to the High Street to breakfast at the bride's father's house.
3/4/1870

AT Bow Street, yesterday, Ernest Boulton, Frederick William Park, and another young man were charged before Mr Flowers with frequenting a place of public resort – to wit, the Strand Theatre – with intent to commit felony, the first two named in female attire. On being placed in the dock, much amusement was created by their artistic make-up. Boulton was dressed in fashionable crimson silk, trimmed with white lace. He wore a flaxen wig with plaited chignon. His arms and neck were bare. He had bracelets, and a white lace shawl round his shoulders. Park wore a green satin dress, with panier, flaxen wig curled, white kid gloves, bracelets, and black lace shawl. A long examination took place, and the evidence of the police proved that the two fellows, "gentlemen" in female attire, had for some time been watched, and through their disgraceful conduct were at last taken into custody. Eventually Mr Flowers remanded the prisoners, but allowed the person in male attire to be liberated on his own recognisances of £100. He refused, however, to accept bail for Boulton and Park.
1/5/1870

THE BABY SHOW AT HIGHBURY BARN.
"Merry Islington" has during the past week been inundated with babies. Setting aside the pretty little "squabble" of our French and Prussian neighbours*, babies have been, *par excellence*, the topic of the week, and we have alternately had our attention called to babydom as sacrificed by the convenient machinery of our Brixton baby farmers, and to babydom in all its glory as exhibited by the one hundred mothers who have daily taken their seats in Mr Giovanelli's spacious banqueting hall, anxious to display the merits of that offspring which in more than one case has come like misfortunes, "not singly, but in battalions," that is, two and three at a time.

In two double rows we found the mothers and the babes, some old (that is the mothers), some young, some graced with Nature's fairest gifts, some, like Pharoah's kine, "lean and unfavoured," but all proud and boastful of the adipose lumps of humanity which crowed and nestled in their arms, and revelled occasionally in the delights of that curious compound known as "pap". To babies as a rule, and especially very young babies (forgive us, ye doting mothers!), we are not partial, and, like John Wesley, we like to hear them cry, for then "there is a chance of them being put to bed." But the babies here had evidently submitted to sundry rehearsals for the occasion, and "crying" was conspicuous by its absence.

Of the merits of the juveniles exhibited we venture only to speak under the shield of the anonymous, having the fear of the proud matrons of Highbury before our eyes. "Two little Niggers" first engaged our attention. The first, John Mason, aged eleven months, and weighing 29lbs., was a fine specimen of "black humanity," whose mother's face was of the ordinary English type, and white. The other was a small specimen of three months, and was certainly too young and too small for public introduction. The prettiest child in the Show was No. 14, aged eight months, weight 30lbs. This fair-haired girl was – at least to us – the attraction of the show, and although not boasting a large experience of babies, we should certainly be disposed to award it the first prize for beauty, symmetry, and good temper. No. 41 was a mass of fat, aged four months, with an astonishing proclivity for sucking both its thumbs. No. 1 was a precocious youth of four months and fourteen days, whose parrot-like "gabble" attracted much attention. No. 65 is rightly described as a sleeping beauty. This was Amelia Ward, from Ireland, whose mother took particular care to impress upon our mind the fact that there are no finer children than the

Irish. No. 95, nine months, was chiefly noticeable for its profusion of black hair, and this the mother, who had been married nine years, proudly exhibited as "my first."

We took particular care in this curious and remarkable exhibition to inquire into the treatment which the exhibitors received at the hands of the Management during the six hours they have been daily "on view," and the "good dinner" was the theme of admiration on all sides. The prizes were awarded on Thursday, but the result has not reached us in time for press. Without expressing an opinion upon the advisability of such exhibitions, we may say that every care has been taken by Mr Giovanelli to make his show attractive, and to prove to baby-loving Britons that the rising generation is in no fear of degenerating.

*The Franco-Prussian War, 1870-71.
17/7/1870

WE confess to a liking for little Theatres. There is no necessity for constantly holding an opera-glass to our eyes to distinguish the features of the performers; there is no necessity for the heroine to sprawl and scream in order to attract the attention of the house; the prompter is enabled to do his spiriting gently, and not give secret information to half the orchestra stalls because the rest of the audience are such a long way off; it does not take three-quarters of an hour to arrange the set pieces, and the stage has not the appearance of Salisbury Plain in winter when the chief character has a soliloquy to utter.
11/9/1870

PROSECUTION OF STROLLING PLAYERS AT BRENTFORD.
At the Brentford Petty Sessions on Saturday last Edward Wildman, Proprietor of the Prince of Wales Portable Theatre, and Lucy Ann Mary Sykes, Catherine Ellen Keeley, Joseph Johnson, Montague Keeley, and Henry Rogers, actors, were summoned at the instance of the Commissioner of Police for presenting a stage play in a building not specially licensed for that purpose at Hounslow on the night of the 5th November. The whole of the defendants pleaded not guilty.

Police-constable Ernest Ellisson, 260 T, deposed – Last Saturday night, the 5th inst., I visited a booth which I found erected on the fair-field, Hounslow. I saw a raised stage, foot-lights, a proscenium, scenes, wings, and a drop-curtain. A nautical drama, in three acts, was being performed there. Each of the defendants, dressed in stage costume, took part in the performance. I paid threepence admission to the Theatre. The building is not licensed that I'm aware of. Cross-examined – Rogers appeared as the Dutch smuggler, Johnson as Ben Boling, and Keeley as the Pirate Captain of the Rattlesnake. Defendant Wildman – "Do you say that you saw foot-lights?" Witness – "No, I was wrong there; I correct myself. The lights were at the side or in front." Defendant – "And that's not the only thing you've said wrong. You are the same policeman that was on to us at Hammersmith. Your Worships, he's been an actor himself, and knows all about it." To witness – "Isn't that true?" Witness – "I have been in the line." Wildman – "Yes, and now you round on us because we are trying to get bread and cheese in the same way. I'll be like you, I think; I'll give up acting, and try the police trick. It pays better, doesn't it?"

The Chairman said defendant must not blame the police officer, as he was simply acting under orders, and executing his duty. No doubt he was ordered on this special duty because he did know something about Theatres. What defendant had to do was to prove that his Theatre was licensed. Wildman – "I admit, Sir, that it is not. I would have it licensed directly if I could, but you have no power to grant a licence to a portable building. We keep our Theatre as respectable as it can be kept, and we barely earn a living for our families. Why, therefore, should we be persecuted in this way?" The Chairman – "But there are laws of the country, and you must not set them at defiance."

Inspector Tarling said he could confirm the defendant's assertion that the Theatre was conducted in a very respectable manner. The Chairman said the Bench were not at all anxious to convict in this case, more especially as they heard such a good character of the Theatre, and because they believed that a poor man's evenings would be better spent, perhaps, in such a Theatre than in a beer-house, but they found that there was no exemption in the Act, and therefore the defendants were liable. Defendant Johnson said "if their Worships would refer to the 23rd clause of the Act they would find that a portable Theatre was exempt." The Clerk (after referring to the section) said – "The defendant was quite right to mention this, but the clause did not go so far as he supposed. It exempted such buildings only when used on a lawful fair day, and in the place appointed for the holding of such a fair."

Defendant Wildman produced a number of such cases where the Proprietors of travelling Theatres had been summoned, from which it appeared that much difference of opinion existed amongst Magistrates, and he stated that he was never interfered with in some towns, but that, on the other hand, he had at times been even honoured with the patronage and presence of Magistrates. The Chairman said "defendant clearly infringed the Act of Parliament, but the Bench would be content to inflict merely a nominal fine. On the other hand, if defendant would like to have any legal point in the case argued, the Bench would be willing to let the case stand over a week to enable him to consult a solicitor." Wildman said "he had enough to do to get bread and cheese, and had no money for lawyers. He had a wife and family to support, besides a sick mother, and all he wanted was to earn an honest living, and to keep himself from either begging or stealing. He had been brought up to the stage, and what else could he turn his hand to? If the Bench must fine him he would have to yield, and, trusting they would only make it a nominal fine, he would leave the matter in their hands."

Defendants were then each fined 1s. Subsequently Wildman made an application for a licence for a permanent building in Brentford, but the Clerk informed him of the preliminary measures which he would have to adopt. It was understood that the idea was ultimately abandoned.

20/11/1870

INDEX

ABORIGINAL AUSTRALIANS: to tour as cricketers and entertainers, 66
ACROBAT: does not use cruelty to children, 54; driven mad by cruel practical joke, 38; fatal fall from Nelson Monument near Yarmouth, 20
ACROBATS: Bedouin Arabs, 54
ACTOR: arrested for begging, 64; attempts suicide because of poverty, 20; burns costumes and props after religious conversion, 30; escapes death penalty, 2; fights off thief, 76; narrowly escapes being crushed by heavy prop train, 81; overcharged for breakfast in York, 86; performance as drunk too convincing, 87; threatens to kill police inspector, 1; threatens to whip unruly audience, 64
ACTRESS: accidentally shot, 77; denies playing Shylock, 81; dies of burns, 35 dies suddenly whilst working as theatre attendant, 31; falls down stairs with fearful velocity, 3; has hysterics on stage due to death threat, 14; launches attack on Liverpool press, 14; pierced in oblique direction, 57; pregnant and unmarried, 71; slips on cucumber rind, 14
ACTRESS/LESSEE: robbed by aggressive actor, 33
ADVERTISING: horses frightened by billboard men, 79; humorous, 32; magic transparent cards, 62
ALDRIDGE, IRA (actor): feted in Constantinople, 37
ALMOND ESSENCE: not poisonous, 80
AMATEUR ACTOR: accused of picking nose on stage, 78; outraged by poor review of his Othello, 39
AMATEUR ACTORS: compensated by railway company for non-arrival of costumes, 59; rob professional actors of work, 67; undeservedly praised by press, 23
BABIES: abandoned at theatre, 83
BABY SHOW: rivals Franco-Prussian War as topic of conversation, 93
BALLET DANCER: child of starved by nurse, 2; dies of burns, 17
BALLET DANCERS: dangers of profession, 69; employed in New York under false pretences, 41
BALLOON: destroyed by spontaneous combustion, 70; escapes from mooring, 83; shaped like fish, 50; smashes through stone walls, 12
BAND, military: engagement ends in tragedy, 40
BARBERS: rival, 61
BARMAN: discovered to be barmaid, 51; impudent, 90
BARONET: female: 48
BEAUTIFUL LIZZIE: has leet flaxy hair, 41
BECKWITH, Professor: swims on stage with his amphibious family, 66
BIGAMY: Mrs Rickaby and her four husbands, 68

BIRDS, mechanical: surpass real thing, 52
BLIND TOM: musical prodigy, 39
BOOTH, C.A. (velocipedist): plays instrument and performs magic tricks whilst riding velocipede, 84; rides from London to Brighton in record time, 84
BROWNING, Robert (poet): falsely accused of ordering two bottles of port wine, 59
CHARACTER VOCALIST: does not appear in character, 63
CHICKENS, gigantic: spit fireworks at pantomime performers, 3
CHROMATIC TEA-POT: ideal for those who wish to be musical in a short time, 55
CIGAR, self-lighting: reduces risk of fire, 82
CIRCUS GROOM: killed during performance, 42
CIRCUS MANAGER: charged with assaulting girl apprentice, 24; refuses to pay mule-riding daredevil, 4
CLINTON, Lord Arthur: unable to appear in play due to bereavement, 53
CLOWN: murdered in Constantinople, 8
COMEDIAN: fall leads to death from ruptured liver, 25; invents paper life buoy, 51; pays to attend own performance, 88
COMIC SINGER: giant, 48
CONJUROR: seeks sensible man with £20, 16
COPYRIGHT PROTECTION: British authors suffer from lack of in USA, 56
CROWDING IN THEATRES: causes death of boy at pantomime performance, 61; results in death of shoeblack, 21; twenty people crushed to death on staircase of Dundee concert hall, 29
CRYSTAL PALACE: unsuitable for poetry readings, 19
CURTAIN-RAISERS: senseless trash, 77
DECAPITATION TRICK: too appalling for Leeds, 72
DIVORCE CASE: more than usually scandalous, 45
DOG, performing: awarded medal for saving man from drowning, 5; dies and is stuffed, 70; saves Dundee boy from drowning, 41
DOGS, performing: Brothers Bow Wow, 74; excel as Clowns, 72
DONATO (one-legged dancer): performs shawl dance, 28
DONKEY, pantomime: both halves awarded silver medals, 45
DOUBLING: carried to extremes in *Hamlet*, 88
DRAWERS, bathing without: clergyman found guilty of, 52
DYED SOCKS: injurious to feet, 86
ELEPHANT: has admirable pantomimic powers, 1
ENCORES: undeserved: 31, 37
EQUESTRIENNE, apprentice: bites fellow-apprentice's thigh and absconds, 15; elopes with bounding Arab, 11
EQUESTRIENNES: elopement of sisters, 54
FIRE: false alarm in theatre, 26
FIRE-PROOFING: attempt to make costumes and props impervious to fire, 32
FOOTLIGHTS: ingenious new design at Liverpool theatre, 40
GANDERS: pull Mr Gosford's aquatic chariot, 51
GERMAN BAND: illegality of encouraging, 77
GHOST IN 'HAMLET': takes curtain call, 90
GYMNAST: commits suicide in prison cell, 68
HAIR DYE: secret of rediscovered after almost two thousand years, 50
HISSING: right to hiss indisputable, 49
HORSE: almost crushes orchestra conductor, 83
HOWARD, Lydia ("the Baby Actress"): performs in a scene from *King John* at the age of two, 35; plays Little Red Riding Hood at the age of five, 70
ILLUSIONIST: chemist accidentally sells explosive chemicals to wife of, 26
'JOLLY DOGS' (song): copyright infringement results in court case, 34
LADYBIRDS: swarm in Ramsgate, 86
LETTER-WRITING: unrealistic depiction of by actors, 82
LINCOLN, Abraham: assassination of deplored by actor, 33

LIONS: presence on train disconcerts passengers, 5
LITTLE RED RIDING HOOD: cannot forgive Wolf for eating Grandmother, 62
LIVING SKELETON: is jocular, healthy and intelligent, 35
MARE, hairless: delights audiences, 69
MAY, Samuel (costumier): sells faded finery, 15; wife dies in horrific accident, 55
MISS HERBERT (actress and drama teacher): has titled relations, 70, 71
MONKEY: eats circus takings, 7
MOREAL, RELL: combs his hair with red hot iron, 48
MRS GENERAL TOM THUMB: presented with miniature sewing machine, 28
MUSIC HALL: alarming explosion caused by bursting gas bags, 92; collapses within a few months of opening, 81; false fire alarm panic results in twenty-three deaths at Manchester, 73
MUSIC HALL MANAGER: imposed upon by pregnant and incompetent singer, 24, 25:
NAPOLEON III: French Consul objects to depiction of on poster, 65
NATATOR (human frog): swims with fish, 67
OPERA SINGER: accidentally hits tenor's nose with mallet, 12
PANTALOON: accidentally shot by Clown, 13; attempts suicide because of disappointment in love, 7
PATTI, Adelina (opera singer): faked illness disappoints admirers, 85
PEPPER: causes havoc at ball, 45
PICKPOCKET: operates in theatre, 19
POLICE OFFICER: punched by Amazonian playgoer, 6
PUB LANDLORD: falls foul of law by staging plays on premises, 8
"PUFFING": insult to actors' dignity, 91
PUNCH AND JUDY SHOW: dismal failure in Oxford, 11
SCENE PAINTER: fails to represent London landmarks correctly, 90; poisoned by green paint, 4
SANDFORD, Miss Edith: rides horse through real fire from the stage to the flies, 80
SEAL, performing: plays the triangle, 53
SHEEP: talented, 37
SMALLEST MAN IN THE WORLD: seeks job as barman, 87
SPIRIT-RAPPING: exposed on stage, 14
SPRITE, pantomime: ill-treatment of sons leads to fracas, 13
STAGE HAND: killed by fall through trap door, 29
STAGE HANDS: refuse to catch pantomime Clown, 60
STROLLING PLAYERS: fall foul of law at Hounslow, 94
STUDENT: throws dead rat in playgoers' faces, 7
THEATRE: attempt to blow up, 52; destroyed by fire, 57
THEATRE LESSEE: knocks actress' teeth out in violent assault, 82; mistakes laudanum for brandy, 41
THEATRE MANAGER: cheated out of money by actors, 27; has on-stage fight with violinist, 62; refuses to pay amateur strongman, 4; takes theatre under false pretences, 75
THEATRE TICKETS: alteration of results in court case, 21
TIGHTROPE WALKER: doubles as Shakespearean actor, 10; injured by fall, 72; killed by fall, 16; misrepresentation of act disappoints audience member, 89
TOLMAQUE, Herr (escapologist): objects to being bound by explorer Captain Burton, 27
TRANSVESTITES: arrested outside London theatre, 93
TRAPEZE ARTIST: badly injured by fall into orchestra pit, 65
TRAPEZE ARTISTS: not really brothers, 48
TROUSERS: can be purchased after dark, 80
WAXWORKS DISPLAY, travelling: local residents tormented by noise caused by, 26
WIDOWER, intellectual: sought by lady of independent means, 50
WINDER'S COLOURED FIRES: a boon to workmen in flies and asthmatics in audience, 37

ABOUT THE AUTHOR

Julia D Atkinson was born in Bradford, West Yorkshire, in 1960. She was formerly a critic for the British Theatre Guide. Her ground-breaking article *A name not just now familiar to ears polite:* The Importance of Being Earnest *and* Lady Windermere's Fan *on tour, 1895-1900*, was published in the July 2015 issue of *The Wildean: A Journal of Oscar Wilde Studies*. She now lives in York.

From the same author in the "*Comic and Curious Clippings From the Legendary Theatrical Paper* The Era" series:

A Complete Somersault Into The Orchestra: 1870-1880
Please Throw Two Carrots At Your Mother: 1880-1890
Fairies In Cabs: 1890-1900
Crocodiles In The Green Room: 1900-1910

www.ingramcontent.com/pod-product-compliance
Lightning Source LLC
Chambersburg PA
CBHW081459070526
44586CB00019B/2429